Cultivating Global Citizens

The Edwin O. Reischauer Lectures, 2008

Cultivating Global Citizens

POPULATION IN THE
RISE OF CHINA

Susan Greenhalgh

HARVARD UNIVERSITY PRESS

Cambridge, Massachusetts, and London, England · 2010

Library of Congress Cataloging-in-Publication Data

Greenhalgh, Susan.
    Cultivating global citizens : population in the rise of China / Susan Greenhalgh.
        p. cm. — (Cultivating global citizens. The Edwin O. Reischauer Lectures, 2008.)
    Includes bibliographical references and index.
    ISBN 978-0-674-05571-1 (alk. paper)
    1. China—Population policy. 2. China—Population. 3. China—Social
conditions. 4. China—Politics and government. 5. Birth control—China.
6. Family size—Government policy—China. I. Title.

    HB3654.A3G74   2010
    363.90951—dc22   2010009380

For MEG

Contents

Preface   ix

1 From Population to Human Governance   1

2 Creating Global Persons and a Global Society   37

3 Strengthening China's Party-State and Place in the World   79

Notes   115

Index   131

Preface

China's phoenix-like rise on the global stage is already one of the major stories of the twenty-first century. Not only Chinese-made products, but also Chinese people, ideas, and ways of doing things are circulating around the world, changing their hosts in unexpected ways. While the People's Republic of China (PRC) has been a rising economic power for several decades, students of China's international relations detect a significant change over the last ten years in how the party-state is positioning the nation in world affairs. Building on its extraordinary economic development of recent decades, since the late 1990s, they suggest, an increasingly self-confident China has been exerting influence on global affairs more openly, trying to shape world affairs rather than simply reacting to them. While quietly building up its "hard power" of economic and military resources at home, it has been engaging in a global "charm offensive," as the journalist Joshua Kurlantzick puts it, cultivating its "soft power" to influence people around the world with the appeal of its culture and ideas. A rising Beijing hopes to be perceived as a globally responsible power and on occasion to see its ideals, especially concerning good governance and the good society, become increasingly influential. In ways both planned and not planned by the state, China is becoming an ever-greater presence—and force—in the world in which we live.

What does the cultivation of China's society have to do with all this? Not much, according to existing accounts. Current analyses of China's global ascent emphasize the economics and the politics, largely neglecting the governance of China's population. Chinese intellectuals, by contrast, recognize the centrality of population to China's rise. The noted political thinker Zheng Bijian has cautioned that current efforts to boost China's national power are haunted by two mathematical propositions: all problems, no matter how small, must be multiplied by 1.32 billion (at the end of 2007); at the same time, all economic gains and resources, no matter how vast, must be divided by 1.32 billion. Suddenly, China's problems have become monumental, while its achievements have become meager. But, as Zheng knows well, population is more than numbers; it is also, in the Chinese term, the "quality" *(suzhi)* of China's people, a broad construct that embraces education, health, ethics, civic values, and global savvy, attributes that are increasingly collected under the term "human capital." In the late 1970s, at the very time it launched its economic program of "reform and opening up," the PRC regime inaugurated a massive project on population designed to create a high-quality, competitive workforce and a modern citizenry befitting a global power. That project to shrink the quantity and upgrade the quality of China's people has accomplished some of its laudable goals, but it has produced just as many unintended, sometimes very troubling, effects as well. For better and for worse, that project on population has left a deep imprint on the China that is emerging on the world stage.

The governance of China's population is also absent from many accounts of recent transformations in Chinese society and politics. Although some anthropological and sociological studies of social change—especially those focusing on gender, sexuality, health, and youth—do highlight the centrality of population policy, other accounts of social change, including many dealing with the making of modern Chinese selves, ignore it. Population is notably absent from most political science work on Chinese politics and China's party-state. Perhaps because "population" belongs to "demography," many leading texts on China's party-state and elite politics simply omit population and the politics surrounding it. If population is included, it tends to appear in a (usually brief) discussion of social policy. Or it shows up in a discussion of rural politics, where it is reduced to family planning and used to illustrate societal resistance to state control.

It is not only the division of intellectual labor in the social sciences that has given population such a low profile in accounts of contemporary Chinese politics. Equally if not more important is the grip on our imaginations of one particular, narrowly framed narrative about China, one that emphasizes state coercion of society above all else. Rooted in cold war realities, the coercion narrative sees the PRC birth and population program as a manifestation of a brutal totalitarian state forcing society to limit its childbearing, provoking societal resistance on a massive scale. For several decades now, the coercion account has served as a master narrative, deeply imprinting

Western—and perhaps especially American—academic, journalistic, political, and legal discourse on China's population politics. By keeping us riveted on only one feature of China's population work, and a feature that is fading with time, the coercion story has been diverting our attention from other critical dimensions of population work and from the transformations in China's population affairs that are underway today. If we are to understand this rising global power, and understand how we as Americans might most effectively respond, we need new ways to think about China's population project and how it has reshaped China's society and politics.

To see the centrality of population, we need to look more closely at the role of science and technology, and of knowledge more generally, in Chinese political life. There now exists a relatively large literature on China's science policy, and a small but growing body of work on the rise of China's technocratic state. Yet little has been written about how the political incorporation of techno-scientific logics has shaped the way the PRC regime governs its people. Modern scientific/engineering logics and techniques are particularly important in the field of population politics, because population is framed as a biological entity that can be governed only through "science."

In this book I suggest new ways to think about China's ambitious project on population. I approach these issues as an anthropologist and ethnographer interested in the making of modern persons and modern societies. My reframing of the problem of population governance draws on two bodies of political thought that are influential in anthropology at large, but have only recently been applied to the study of China: governmentality studies, which emphasizes governing logics, and science and technology studies, which highlights the political nature and effects of modern science and technology. I argue that since the outset of the reform period, the People's Republic has witnessed the emergence of a new mode of governing its people, one that works through modern science and technology, focuses on the biological body at aggregate and individual levels, and aims to both speed and optimize China's transformation into a global power. Population politics—a domain I call biopolitics or vital politics—has been central to the globalizing agenda of the reform regime. By helping to transform China's rural masses into modern workers and citizens; by working to strengthen, techno-scientize, and legitimize the PRC regime; and by boosting China's economic development and comprehensive national power, the biogovernance of the population has been vitally important to the rise of global China.

Over the first decade of the new millennium, in part because China has been abandoning the brutal practices that undergirded the familiar coercion narrative, there has been a sharp fall-off of international media interest in that nation's population affairs. Ironically, even as the management of population is becoming a larger part of Chinese governance generally, it is quietly receding as a focus of media and thus general public interest in the United States. I hope to restore public and scholarly interest in China's project of population cultivation by refocusing attention from its coercive methods to its globalizing objectives.

Drawing on governmentality and science studies, in this book I broaden the field of population politics beyond a conventional focus on institutions to include discourse, science, subjectivity, and the body as objects of critical inquiry. Using this more expansive view of what counts as population governance suggests that population has played a much larger role in China's politics and state-making than is generally appreciated. In the PRC, this enlarged perspective suggests, population—in particular, the notion that there are "too many Chinese"—is a fundamental source of cultural and national identity, a prominent political fact, and a central domain of state policy and politics at every level from the political Center to the locality. (By political Center I mean the cluster of party and governmental institutions in which power is centralized in the PRC; Chinese citizens refer to these institutions simply as "the center," or *zhongyang*.)

Indeed, in the reform era, population politics has been central to China's party-state in a number of ways, which have shifted over time. I will argue that in the 1980s and 1990s, the population project helped to strengthen the state's governing capacity, boost the party's legitimacy, and produce a steady stream of new techniques of social governance. In the first decade of the new millennium, population governance has been a major site for experimentation with and adoption of the new, more indirect, "human-centered" techniques of governance that have become the hallmark of the Hu Jintao–Wen Jiabao administration (2003–). The embrace of such techniques—which, like the neoliberal methods of good governance used elsewhere, work in part by promoting more entrepreneurial, self-directed private selves—has helped the party-state defy predictions of its decline and eventual disintegration, instead fostering the view, increasingly articulated by political commentators today, that the PRC regime has proven remarkably resilient in an era of rapid marketization. Finally, looking into the future, as China continues its shift from its earlier focus on rapid gross domestic product (GDP) growth at any cost toward addressing the social costs of that economy-first model, the management of population—which is now evolving into social policy—can be expected to become ever more central to governance generally.

Taking population science and politics into account also changes conventional stories about the making of modern Chinese selves and society. It suggests that today's rise of the self-optimizing, self-governing subject is rooted not only in the expansion of the market, but also in deliberate policy choices by the state. The private selves emerging in today's globalizing economy are highly differentiated, and some of those distinctions are produced by the state's efforts to create varied kinds of persons needed for the success of its globalization project. State efforts to normalize China's society to modern, global standards have also remade society as a whole, fostering a quantitatively and qualitatively "modern, global society," while at the same time labeling large categories of individuals as "backward" or "deviant," and excluding them from the state's regime of social welfare and social virtue. The state's project of rapid reproductive modernization has also created a huge gap between the genders and accelerated the problem of aging without social security, leaving legacies of inequality that will haunt China's people and its planners for decades to come.

The ideas developed here emerge from long-term ethnographic engagement with China's population policy and politics that has extended well over twenty years. This research, described in other publications, has taken me to both traditional and nontraditional research sites at virtually every level of the political system, from the political Center down to the village. I did extended fieldwork in three villages in the northwestern province of Shaanxi, as well as shorter-term field research in experimental villages in several provinces, provincial statistical offices, municipal birth planning offices, and township clinics. I did not do fieldwork among ordinary citizens in any of China's cities; for their stories, I draw on the work of colleagues in urban anthropology. My research also involved often lengthy interviews with population officials and scholars, documentary research on the history of Chinese population science and policy, and ethnographic research on Chinese policy science conducted while working collaboratively with Chinese researchers in the 1980s and early 1990s. I think of the result of these various engagements as a sprawling, multisited, multilevel ethnography of the Chinese party-state or, more precisely, of a party-state project of social governance. Because of space constraints, in this book I step back from the detailed empirical material to draw out larger analytic themes. Readers interested in accounts of individuals and other ethnographic specifics might wish to consult some of my other writings.

These essays were originally presented as the 2008 Edwin O. Reischauer Lectures of Harvard's Fairbank Center for Chinese Studies. One of the great virtues of the Reischauer Lectures is their emphasis on intra-Asian comparison and contrast. In a discussion of Asian populations, one expects a pairing of China and India, those demographic billionaires whose population policies present striking contrasts between "democratic" and "authoritarian" ways of doing things (though India has engaged in its share of authoritarianism, too). And, indeed, there have been many such comparative studies. Here I approach the project of intra-Asian comparison differently. As an ethnographer of a governmental project of the PRC regime, one of my primary concerns is to understand that project and its larger goals from the vantage point of China's leaders. I want to get inside their heads and see what they hoped to achieve with their massive efforts to trim the growth and upgrade the quality of China's people. My concern with other nations, then, centers on how they figure in the party-state's project of global advance through population limitation and cultivation. As we will see, since around 1980, China's extraordinary efforts to modernize its population have been part of an overarching national venture to boost China's global influence, standing, and power. In assessing its "comprehensive national power"—the key objective—China measures its own greatness against four other countries. These include two Asian giants—India and Japan—as well as Russia, its old nemesis, and the sole global superpower, the United States. In these pages my comparative observations thus focus primarily on these countries. I track how China ranks relative to these perceived competitors in terms of population quantity and quality, and the importance of aggregate measures of "human development" or "human capital" in boosting China's overall power relative to these other big countries.

These essays build on ideas first presented in two recent books, while taking them in new directions. *Governing China's Population: From Leninist to Neoliberal Biopolitics,* written with Edwin A. Winckler (2005) (hereafter

GCP), traces the "governmentalization" of population from 1949 to 2004, a process in which first the state and later also society and the market have been increasingly involved in managing and perfecting China's population. *Just One Child: Science and Policy in Deng's China* (2008) unearths the origins of the one-child policy in Deng-era science and politics. In this book, I bring the story of China's remarkable politics of population up to early 2009 in a format that I intend to be concise and accessible. I leave theory in the background to focus on several new themes. The most prominent, of course, is the role of population governance in China's global rise. I pay particular attention to the new forms of social and human governance that have gained prominence in the years since GCP was written; to the emergence of new types of more self-directed, market calculating persons; and to the place of population in China's ambitious schemes to boost its overall national strength. Although my focus is the immediate post-2000 period, and especially the years 2004 to 2009, I also summarize developments during 1980 to 2000. This material provides an essential historical backdrop, helping us to understand how much things have changed, why they have changed, and why the transformations underway today are so significant.

I am deeply grateful to the Fairbank Center for Chinese Studies for the opportunity to share my ideas with members of the Asian studies community at Harvard. Particular thanks go to Marty Whyte, Acting Director of the Center and Professor of Sociology, and Ron Suleski, Assistant Director of the Center, who invited me to deliver the lectures, organized the talks, and provided for my every need. I am indebted to my discussants—Professor Hue-Tam Ho Tai, Kenneth T. Young Professor of Sino-Vietnamese History at Harvard; Danièle Bélanger, Associate Professor of Sociology and Canada Research Chair in Population, Gender, and Development at the University of Western Ontario; and Anthony Saich, Daewoo Professor of International Affairs at Harvard's Kennedy School of Government—for provocative questions and comments that made me see my topic in new ways. A personal thanks goes to Marty Whyte, James (Woody) Watson, and Rubie Watson, who chaired the three lecture sessions with humor and warmth and created a special opportunity for me to meet and engage with their students in China anthropology. Finally, a note of appreciation goes to the Harvard Asian studies community at large for an exceptionally warm welcome and stimulating experience.

Cultivating Global Citizens

1

From Population to Human Governance

My subject—how China governs its population and to what effect—is one of the most difficult in the study of contemporary China. Although state efforts to regulate reproduction are sensitive issues everywhere, since the early 1980s, China's tough one-child-per-couple policy and harsh enforcement methods have generated political controversy and ethical conflict around the world. Despite the recurring criticisms from abroad, Chinese population planners have forged ahead, claiming great success in lowering fertility and boosting China's—and the world's—sustainable development.

As a result of official program efforts—and, equally important, supercharged economic growth—in the years since 1979–1980, when the one-child policy was introduced, fertility has fallen from just under 3 to 1.5–1.6 children per woman. Fertility levels in China, which is still a relatively poor country, match those of the much richer West, where average childbearing rates range from 1.3 to 1.4 in Italy, Russia, and Japan, to 2.1 in the United States.[1] This rapid decline in Chinese fertility, however, has incurred wrenching social costs, costs that include not only the human trauma and social suffering of those subjected to state coercion, but also a growing gender gap among newborns and rapid aging in a context that is largely lacking public forms of social security. At 120 boys per 100 girls, China's sex ratio at birth is now the highest in the world. At the other end of the age spectrum, the number of Chinese elderly without adequate economic support and health insurance is projected to explode after 2015, throwing huge numbers of older Chinese into poverty and threatening China's continued global ascent.

Despite these destabilizing social trends, the one-child policy remains firmly in place. (I use the conventional term "one-child policy" because the state advocates one for all and uses strong sanctions to enforce the policy. Since the mid-1980s, some categories of couples, especially rural couples whose first child is a girl, and couples comprised of two singletons, have been allowed to have two children.)[2] In 2001, official "advocacy" *(tichang)* of single-child families was for the first time embedded in national law. In January 2007, the one-child norm was reaffirmed in an important new decision of the party Central Committee and governmental State Council. In March 2008, China's minister of population and birth planning announced that the policy would remain in place for at least ten more years, silencing rumors of a policy adjustment to ease the damaging effects of the masculinization and accelerated aging of China's society.[3] Although some localities with exceptionally low fertility have been allowing couples made up of two singletons to have two children—Shanghai, the leader in this effort, has been pushing the limit by actively encouraging such couples to have two— advocacy of one-child families remains the official, politically sanctioned law of the land.[4]

Since the mid-1980s, when the Western media began to expose the human costs of the one-child policy, China's approach to governing its population has been understood in this country as first and foremost a matter of communist coercion. In this narrative, a brutal totalitarian state forces China's people to limit their childbearing against their will, provoking resistance, and, when the state strikes back, terrible social suffering. With its twin emphases on state force and state–society struggle the coercion account is fundamentally one of the means—not the ends—of the Chinese program. As one of the most overarching, pervasive stories about China, the coercion account has served as a master narrative that has deeply influenced the way we think and talk about China's population work.

This story has dominated media, political, and even scholarly accounts of China's population politics. In the scholarly literature on China, that nation's rural population politics, and Chinese population politics more generally, have commonly been portrayed as an unending struggle between a coercive state and a resistant society that continues to this day.[5] The image of China as a coercive violator of reproductive rights also appears in the comparative literature on population politics. In *Fatal Misconception,* a critical history of the international family planning movement, historian Matthew Connelly makes China the poster child for all the flaws of that movement, which he maintains was a "tragic mistake" because it relied on coercing individuals rather than empowering them to shape their own reproductive destinies.[6]

Because this story has so powerfully shaped the way we as scholars and as Americans perceive China, it is crucial to begin our analysis with that account, examining how it was born and grew to be so influential, and what kinds of cognitive work it has performed. Readers wishing to get right to the story of China itself might prefer to skip this section for now and return to it later.

The Rise and Long Life of the Coercion Story

The coercion account of China's population politics was born and flourished in the cold war era—the 1950s through 1970s—when "Red China" was the "totalitarian other," the foil to the democratic West. The coercion story about population both draws on and, in turn, contributes to a larger cultural narrative that makes state coercion and societal resistance defining features of life in Communist China.

The mass media played a central role in constructing and later embellishing the story. In the decades following World War II, the *New York Times* and the *Washington Post,* this country's most influential newspapers, published scores of articles on China's population control efforts, the vast majority of which described a cruel communist state suppressing the reproductive desires of the Chinese people. A sampling of titles of these articles can be found in Table 1. In the early post-1949 years (roughly the mid-1950s, when birth control was instituted, to 1978), reporters based in Hong Kong detailed the emergence of harsh government restrictions on childbearing, depicting a Red China that "presses," "pushes," "decrees," and "intensifies" official curbs on population. In 1979, when American reporters gained access to the PRC itself, they elaborated the story to include dogged peasant resistance to the new one-child policy, state–society struggles over its implementation, and the tragic consequences for China's people: "castaway babies," the "killing of baby girls," and "millions of missing women."

The sheer number of articles on China's birth program suggests a journalistic preoccupation if not obsession with the Chinese approach to population governance. During the period of harshest enforcement of the one-child

Table 1 The Coercion Story in the *New York Times* and *Washington Post*, Mid-1950s to 1993

Mid-1950s to 1978: Harsh Policy and Enforcement
  Birth Control Use in China is Pressed (*NYT*, 9/25/56)
  Peiping to Decree Population Curbs (*NYT*, 3/8/57)
  Reds Silence Defiant Head of Peking University [who advocated population control]
    (*WP*, 4/17/60)
  Red China Decries Early Marriages: Young People are Warned in Move to Cut Births
    (*NYT*, 6/3/62)
  Peking Opens a New Drive to Limit Population (*NYT*, 6/16/63)
  Birth Control Pushed by Reds in Shanghai (*WP*, 7/4/63)
  Peking Urges Birth Curbs: Big Families are Penalized (*NYT*, 4/27/66)
  China Intensifies Population Curbs. Sterilization and Delayed Marriages Encouraged
    (*NYT*, 7/6/66)
  Chinese Reds Condemn Those Young People Who "Idle Away their Time" Planning
    Early Marriage (*NYT*, 9/15/68)
  China's People: A Job for the Birth Control Teams (*NYT*, 2/20/72)
  Peking is Pressing New Campaign to Control Births (*NYT*, 1/28/73)
  China is Pressing Birth-Curb Drive: Effort Backed by Mao Aims to Limit Desire for Sons
    and Population Rise (*NYT*, 9/8/75)
  Sterilization Frequently Used in China's Program (*WP*, 12/12/76)
  Chinese Said to Determine Sex of Fetus, Abort Females (*WP*, 3/1/77)
  China Reports Setback in Effort to Curb Population Growth (*WP*, 12/7/78)

1979–1993: Resistance, Crackdown, and the Human Consequences
  A Tough New Drive on Births in China (*NYT*, 10/10/79)
  Chinese Reds Limited to a Child per Family (*NYT*, 9/27/80)
  "One Baby Only" (*WP*, 10/19/80)
  China's Birth Goals Meet Regional Resistance (*NYT*, 5/15/82)
  China Plans a New Drive to Limit Birth Rate (*NYT*, 11/7/82)
  Infanticide in China (*NYT*, 4/11/83)
  China Says Many Defy its Birth Control Policy (*NYT*, 10/9/83)
  China Orders Sterilization for Parents (*WP*, 5/28/83)
  Chinese Statistics Indicate Killing of Baby Girls Persists (*WP*, 7/11/84)
  China's Birth Rate on Rise Again as Official Sanctions are Ignored (*NYT*, 4/21/87)
  China's Population Growth Soars as Couples Skirt "One-Child" Policy (*WP*, 4/3/87)
  The Spoiled Brats of China: Family Policy Produces "Little Emperors" (*WP*, 7/26/87)
  Chinese Population Drive Falters. Government Report Describes Resistance in Countryside
    (*WP*, 1/16/88)
  Chinese Region Uses New Law to Sterilize Mentally Retarded (*NYT*, 11/21/89)
  China Failing to Curb Births: Provinces Implementing Harsher Penalties (*WP*, 12/28/90)
  Changsha Journal. China's Castaway Babies: Cruel Practice Lives On (*NYT*, 2/26/91)
  Stark Data on Women: 100 Million are Missing. A Preference for Boys Dooms Girls,
    Demographers Say; in Asia, the Problem is Getting Worse (*NYT*, 11/5/91)
  Infanticide Continues in Rural China (*WP*, 10/24/91)

Source: Author's research

policy (1979–1993), these two newspapers together carried up to twelve articles a year—one per month—on the Chinese program. (The peak years for items on the birth program were 1979, 1985, 1991, and 1993.) Many in the West, reporters included, were deeply troubled by China's birth program, which seemed to confirm Americans' worst fears about the horrors of a totalitarian state. China's population program was also disturbing because it blatantly violated a fundamental American value: the liberal value of individual freedom from state constraint on reproduction. That core belief in the right to reproductive freedom, coupled no doubt with a sense of ethical repulsion, help explain the broad and enduring appeal of the coercion narrative about China.

The coercion story that had been developing in the media gained critical new impetus in the mid-1980s, when it was taken up by a newly emerging coalition on the right in American politics. In the early to mid-1980s, a new, tight-knit coalition of conservative Republicans and right-to-life advocates, many with strong anti-communist sentiments, made China's population policy their *cause célèbre* in a public crusade against abortion.[7] In 1981, some linked the issue of coercion in the Chinese program to U.S. support for the United Nations Population Fund (UNFPA), which had established a program in Beijing in 1979. The United States, they claimed, should not fund a UN agency that supports coercion in China. The movement gained critical ammunition in early 1985 with the publication in the *Washington Post* of a three-part series that was intensely critical of the one-child policy. Using graphic language and battle metaphors, the articles, by Michael Weisskopf, carried grisly titles: "Shanghai's Curse: Too Many Fight for Too Little; Tough Birth Control Policy Shakes Chinese Society"; "Abortion Policy Tears at China's Society"; and "China's Birth Control Policy Drives Some to Kill Baby Girls."[8]

This New Right coalition claimed the China population control issue as its own, using the Weisskopf articles and other quasi-academic writings to frame the matter as one of brute coercion by a communist state against a defiantly resistant population. Particularly important was the work of John S. Aird, demographer and longtime China watcher at the Census Bureau. Despite their conceptual and empirical limitations, Aird's frequent statements before various congressional committees and his 1989 book, *Slaughter of the Innocents: Coercive Birth Control in China*, were given exceptional credence among influential circles in Washington.[9] The status of Aird's views as "the truth" about China's population politics rested in part on his exclusive reliance on official Chinese sources (which, most scholars believe, are necessary but not sufficient) and in part on the usefulness of his account to the coalition's right-to-life agenda.[10]

In a protracted political struggle, the New Right advanced its cause by constantly expanding the scope of conflict over the China issue—in the mass media, in congressional hearings, in discussions with the White House, and in other public forums. By taking every opportunity to broadly publicize their account, and coloring it with a strong dose of ethical judgment, they were able to make their story the most compelling and familiar account of the Chinese program. In part because the New Right formed a crucial constituency for Ronald Reagan, it gained the support of the president. By the mid-1980s, the coercion story had become not only the most prominent story; it had become the de facto official story about the Chinese program, shaping a number of important U.S. policies toward China. (This story is told later.)

During the 1980s, the debate over the Chinese program was highly polarized. People who supported U.S. funding for UNFPA, and scholars with other, more nuanced analyses of Chinese population politics, were silenced by the constant attacks on their positions, by the claims of the right-wingers to the moral high ground, and by the ad hominem attacks against population professionals who did not loudly condemn China as pawns of the Chinese state.[11] In this highly charged environment, there was no place for any other point of view. Because the coercion narrative fit American preconceptions about China, because it made sense of the facts that were most readily available (those gathered and published by journalists), and because other kinds of accounts were actively suppressed, the coercion narrative became virtually the only extant story about China's population affairs.

The Coercion Story Today

Although the cold war ended long ago, during the George W. Bush years (2001–2009) the coercion account and the broader human rights critique of the Chinese program remained the predominant story on Capitol Hill, where human rights campaigners like Harry Wu and congressmen like

Christopher H. Smith (Republican of New Jersey) continued to ferret out and publicize instances of coercive zeal in program enforcement. China's population control efforts were (and still are) a major item on the Web site of Wu's Laogai Research Foundation (www.laogai.org). A click on "population control" links viewers to a large collection of articles documenting population-related abuses—from the trafficking of children to the party's expulsion of hundreds of members for defying the one-child policy. The message conveyed is that such abuses are the only thing worth noting about how China governs its population. Congressman Chris Smith is well known on the Hill for his frequent statements on China's population policies at congressional hearings. At a hearing in early 2008, for example, he condemned "the government's draconian one child per couple policy . . . which has made brothers and sisters illegal . . . contravenes international human rights standards at every level . . . and has led to a social plague of gendercide, the annihilation of tens of millions of girls, just because they were girls."[12] These critiques remain important—yet, I will argue, they are partial in ways that matter.

In the 2000s, there has been a fall-off in media stories about China's population affairs, a result, no doubt, of the decline in the use of physical coercion in the program since the mid-1990s. Yet when anything important happens on the population front, it is still narrated through (a variant of) the older coercion story. A major focus now is the fate of the one-child policy, which has come to serve as a powerful symbol of the evils of a political system in which a harsh and uncompromising state dictates childbearing. The early 2008 media dustup about the one-child policy is telling. In late February, Reuters quoted China's vice minister of population and family planning, Zhao Baige, as saying that China was considering scrapping its controversial policy: "I cannot answer at what time or how, but this has become a big issue among decision makers."[13] Reporters jumped on these remarks, reproducing them, together with expert commentary, in papers all over the world. Zhao's comments provoked an immediate and sharp rebuttal from her boss, Minister of Population and Family Planning Zhang Weiqing, who announced a few days later that "China will by no means waver in its family planning policy anytime soon." Only after the current baby boom ends about a decade from now, he added, will the state consider a major policy adjustment.[14] From this episode we can see that population still holds considerable interest in public debates about China, and that public interest continues to center on the one-child policy.

From State Coercion to China's Global Rise

Public narratives such as this demand close attention because they actively shape what we can see, say, and think about the world around us. The coercion story about Chinese population governance has helpfully drawn our attention to terrible human rights abuses in the Chinese program and the determined resistance mounted by certain categories of Chinese citizens. This focus was critically important in the 1980s and early 1990s, when such abuses were appallingly commonplace. Since then, however, both China and its approach to population work have radically changed. Yet our stories and understandings have not kept up. The persistence of the cold war–era coercion story is important because that story performs critical cognitive work that continues to shape the way we see China. To simplify, the story makes four implicit assertions that color our perceptions. It asserts that: (1) population is about population control—quantity limitation; (2) the state is the most important agent of population governance; (3) the one-child policy is the single most important instrument of population management; and (4) population administration is essentially about the state coercion of society. Power over population is thus fundamentally negative, oppressive, regressive, bad. Put crudely, coercion is the single most important thing we should track in monitoring and analyzing China's population politics.

But is the trampling of Chinese citizens' reproductive rights the most important way China's population policies impinge on us as Americans? This question is worth pondering. Without a doubt, the critique of coercion in the Chinese program is an essential part of our response as Americans schooled in the values and virtues of a liberal society and dismayed by the ethical transgressions it has wrought. Yet an overwhelming emphasis on state coercion and societal resistance constricts our vision and limits our actions in unfortunate ways. What if coercion were not the major way the Chinese program has worked? What if the one-child policy were a small—and increasingly irrelevant—part of how China governs its population? What if the Chinese party-state were not the major "governor" of China's population?

I believe there is a better story, one that incorporates the coercion critique yet embeds it in a more overarching narrative about the rise of a new, largely uncharted field of politics. My aim in this slender volume is to offer new ways to think about China's project of population governance. I will suggest that since the beginning of the reform era, China has witnessed the emergence of a new mode of governing its people, one that works through modern science and technology, focuses on the biological body, and aims to both speed and optimize China's transformation into a global power. Although initially it focused narrowly on quantity control, over time this project of population administration and cultivation has grown ever broader in scope, involving a widening range of state, quasi-state, and nonstate political actors. Since the turn of the millennium, population governance has begun to give way to social and even human governance, bringing a new, more "human-centered" configuration of logics, techniques, and strategic ends to the fore. In the meantime, as these transformations in population governance have been unfolding, population has become a major domain of Chinese policy and governance. The role of population politics has been largely ignored by students of China's ascent, who have focused on the economics and the politics behind that process, reducing population to mere family planning. Yet population deserves our closest attention. By remaking society and politics in particular ways, the governance of population has been vitally important to the rise of global China. My argument is not that the coercion account is wrong—it is not (though it is becoming less relevant today). My argument is that a global-ascent-through-modern-science-and-technology perspective is more useful: it tells us more about the population project—what it entails, how it works, and why it matters. Moreover, it answers key questions about population politics that the coercion story cannot answer. Lastly, it enables a more serious analysis of the consequences of the population project—for China's people, its party–state, and the nation as a whole.

Problems of Concept and Method: Population as Vital Politics

Let's begin with some basics. First, what is population? For most of us, I suspect, population is a narrow, technical topic, to do with numbers and statistics, and best left to the demographers. But there are other, fresh and, I think, stimulating ways to think about population. I approach the subject as an anthropologist and ethnographer interested in the making of modern persons and modern societies. For me, population is first and foremost a field of politics and an object of scientific and governmental attention. Demography—what I prefer to call population science to call attention to its science-ness—is a key actor in that political field, providing logics (theories, historical cases, and the like), techniques (calculations, projections, and so forth), and policy proposals that shape projects on population. Population science is not so much a means by which we investigate the world, then, as an object of ethnographic inquiry in itself.

Population Governance as an Ethnographic Question:
Conceptual Foundations

As an object of science and governance, population functions on two inter-connected levels: the individual and the population as a whole. States and other governing agents try to modernize their populations by getting indi-viduals to adopt their modern norms on sexuality, marriage, contraception, childbearing, and so forth. In anthropological terms, the domain of study is reproductive politics—the negotiations and contests that unfold as govern-ing agents try to get individuals to accept their modern reproductive norms and associated practices. This field is easy to access ethnographically, and indeed, there is a large literature on the politics of reproduction in various sites around the world.

But how can an ethnographer study the population as a whole? How can we get a population to tell its stories, to give up its secrets? It would be diffi-cult to use participant observation, anthropology's classic method, to study a population, which after all is an abstract entity, but one can study that collec-tive entity in at least two interesting ways: as a statistical phenomenon and as a governmental phenomenon. In studying population as a statistical object, one can, for example, examine the numbers, charts, and tables representing "population," looking to see what stories they might tell about a nation's people, their characteristics, pasts, and futures. In examining population as an object of governance, one can pore over the documents produced by states and other governing agents, looking to see how "the problem of population" and its "ideal solution" are rhetorically framed. For example, the problem of population could be (and in various parts of the world is) framed as one of population numbers (fertility, population growth rate, and/or size), citizen health, population distribution, or population structure (by age, sex, race/ ethnicity, and so on). Similarly, demographic worries could center on the damaging consequences for the economy, the environment, national security, or internal political stability. Such framings of "population" are crucial because rarely do they simply reflect a reality that already exists in nature; more often, they also constitute a new reality by shaping what is thinkable in the domain of population. A powerful framing, once it is embedded in public policy and bureaucratically enacted, can remake the world in which we live. The PRC provides dramatic illustration of that point.

These ethnographic projects on population and reproduction were inspired by a broader body of ideas that I map out elsewhere. These ideas emerge from the field of science studies, which examines science in social context, and studies of "governmentality" (a combination of government and political rationality), which explores modes of governing beyond the state. Both draw inspiration from Michel Foucault's groundbreaking work on modern sexuality and governance, while moving his ideas in fresh directions.[15] In his writings on historical Europe, Foucault redefined the field of modern politics and made population central to that field. Although his ideas on population are exceptionally illuminating of contemporary developments, including in China, few have pursued them or explored their full implications for the contemporary world. This is the challenge I take up in my work. Here I provide the briefest of introductions to the ideas I develop below, just enough to ground our inquiry.

In recent years, specialists on modern governance have drawn attention to the historical emergence of a new form of power, one no longer concentrated in the state but increasingly dispersed throughout society in institutions of medicine, education, and the law. Rooted in modern science, modern power centers on, and works through, the biological body, at the individual and collective levels. Following Foucault, this account proposes that, to a growing extent, modern power is power over life, in the biological sense, and modern governance is the governance of human life—that is, the administration and cultivation of individual and collective life, health, and welfare. Foucault called this field "biopolitics." We might call it "vital politics" or "biogovernance," terms that connect our work on population to other work on modes of governing through biology aimed at optimizing human life.

In the post-Mao era, and especially in the last decade, biogovernance has become increasingly central to Chinese governance generally. The Chinese state has declared science and technology, especially the life sciences and their associated biotechnologies, key to solving the domestic problems of a growing population and to boosting China's status as a global power. With the state's aggressive promotion of the commercialized life sciences and biotechnologies has come the rapid rise of Chinese biocapital, the emergence of bioprospecting, and the formation of new kinds of biocitizens in which identity is intimately linked to health status and to market consumption.[16] Relative to these newer, more glamorous or "frontier" fields of biogovernance, population seems musty indeed. Yet in China, population historically was the first major field in which biological governance was developed, and it remains the largest field of vital politics today, affecting the life of every Chinese citizen. Moreover, the rise of some of these newer fields of life science, technology, and governance was stimulated by developments in the original field of biogovernance. The post-1980 rise of Chinese genetics, for example, was spurred by the demands of the one-child policy for "quality" offspring. The state's project on population deserves our closest attention.

The governmentality perspective highlights the political significance of logics or rationalities of governance. The concrete institutions, policies, and enforcement techniques that are the focus of conventional studies of China's population politics are important too, but the underlying logics have analytical precedence, because they shape how those institutions, policies, and enforcement methods develop. Science is the central logic in modern systems of governance, essential to their construction, operation, and effects. Although the larger political effects of science and scientific logics have been relatively neglected, in the governance of population science-based rationales play a particularly critical role. That is because population is construed as a biological entity (displaying such "vital events" as fertility and mortality) and science claims to be the authority on nature, including biology. The use of scientific rationales and techniques for governing population has broad political effects too, which I will describe as we move along.

An Ethnography of the Chinese State's Project on Population:
A Look Ahead

In this book I pose a series of questions suggested by this work on governing the human through biology. Although the chapters ask big questions, I think of this project as an ethnography of the state, or, more accurately, of a state project. It is ethnographic in its empirical roots in ethnographic field methods; its effort to reflect the views of the Chinese actors—in this case, primarily agents of the state and targets of state-directed management; and my attempt to contextualize that project in broad cultural and historical terms.

In the first chapter I trace the historical rise of an institutionalized politics of life, exploring the process by which the production and cultivation of life became core objects of organized power in China. I examine three dimensions of this process. First, how have the problem of population and its solution been framed, and how have those framings changed over time? Second, what were the strategic ends of China's project(s) in vital politics? How has the party's work on population fit into the reform regime's overarching agenda of rapid modernization and global ascent? Third, what logics have guided the rise of population on the political agenda? How important was the logic of population science and why does it matter?

In the second chapter I explore how the population project has interfaced with Chinese society, its intended object, and with what effects. Here again I pose three questions. First, by what techniques has the population establishment sought to modernize Chinese individuals and society? What kinds of modern subjects has the population field sought to create and how have the modes of subject-making changed over time? Second, which political agents have been able to define and instill the norms (or standards) guiding life and thus to "govern" China's population? In Western Europe, the rise of a politics of life was closely tied to the development of capitalism, when healthy bodies and educated minds were required to form a new labor force for the growing economy. With the emergence of capitalism, the power to shape the norms guiding the cultivation of life shifted from the state to other entities, most importantly the educational and medical professions and the market. In Asia, since the late 1970s the PRC has intensified its efforts to shape a modern labor force that is competitive in the global economy. Has rapid integration into the capitalist world economy brought about a similar, state-to-market shift in the power to shape life in that society? Third, what are the broad social effects of the rise of population on the political agenda? Work on modern governance suggests that projects on population rarely achieve their intended goals, but they are productive in other ways. In China the low-quantity–high-quality policies introduced in 1979–1980 were created to modernize Chinese society at individual and collective levels. Is this what they accomplished? What else did they accomplish in the process?

In the final chapter, I examine the broad political effects of China's population project. That project was aimed both at strengthening the regime and at accelerating the PRC's transformation into a global power. Did China's leaders achieve their intended goals? What else did they achieve while seeking those ends?

Problems of "Population": From Economic to Social Governance

Let us turn, then, to the history of population in the PRC. Leading accounts of China's post-Mao population politics tell this story essentially as one of shifts in the rules and enforcement of the one-child policy. This approach assumes that the population problem has always been one of excess numbers, and that the major actors have been China's state and society engaged in a protracted struggle over those numbers. Yet when we listen to China's population officials talk and write about their work, we discover that the problem of population is much bigger and involves many more actors than those analyses have suggested.

Let us set aside the equation of population with excess numbers to ask how the problem(s) of population have actually been understood by China's political leaders and population officials. Using official documents and other materials (leader speeches, news items, information on the Web sites of the population bureaucracies, and the like), I examine how the problem of population has been framed; what logics have underlain these framings; and which political actors have been charged with implementing the solution, and thus governing China's population. How a social problem is officially construed is important, because that formulation decisively shapes the governmental solution. A study of framings answers a very basic question: What even counts as population, what is in the "frame?" In China the party-state has had virtually total control over the naming and framing of the population issue since the early 1950s, when the state claimed population as its own, silencing independent-minded intellectuals. Since that time, through its near hegemonic control of the mass media, the state has largely determined what the citizenry has thought about the nature, scope, urgency, and necessary solution to the nation's population problems.

There is no way to know what the makers of the post-Mao population project in 1979–1980 expected to happen in their domain of governance, but they probably did not imagine that their object, population, would grow and flourish, taking on a life of its own. For China's leaders, "population" turned out to be a versatile and productive object of governance. In a textbook example of what Foucault called the "governmentalization of the state," the construct "population" has given rise to multiple and ever-multiplying problems, which then required governmental solutions.[17] New topics have been brought under the rubric "population" for many reasons. In some cases, leaders expanded the domain to solve problems created by previous approaches. In others, the field was stretched to address new social problems created by massive social and political change more generally. In still others, the terrain was reworked to adapt to developments in the international environment. In yet others, new topics were added in response to new directions of party governance established by top leaders. The result was that a large and growing array of topics was fitted under the rubric of population.

Since the nature of the population problem was constantly being defined and redefined in response to all these forces, it would be impossible in this short book to trace all the permutations that have occurred in the construction of population as a problem of governance. Instead, I examine the framing of the population problem at just two points in time: the beginning of the reform era (1979–1980) and roughly three decades later (2007–2008).

From the outset of the reform era, the management of population has been a key plank in China's strategy to gain competitive advantage in the global order and to rise in the ranking of rich and powerful nations. The population project was *bio*political to the core, involving governing the biological body of the nation through science and technology. Population thus formed the centerpiece of the regime's bionationalist project of capitalist modernization and global advance. Throughout the reform decades, then, population has remained a state-led project directed to nationalist ends. Over the years, however, as the regime's larger strategies of development and globalization have shifted, the approach to population governance has changed. From an exclusively economic problem, population has become an economic, social, and even human problem. We trace those consequential changes here.

Quantity and Quality: Population as a Problem of Economic Governance (1979–1980)

In the decades of socialist construction—roughly the 1950s to the 1970s— the problem of population was framed as an imbalance in the state development plan. From the mid-1950s, when population became a matter of party-state concern, the main problem of population was quantity: the excessive growth of Chinese numbers hindered the party's plans for rapid industrialization and socialist construction. The solution was to lower population growth by encouraging late marriage and few births. The method, proposed by Mao himself, was the state planning of births nationwide. This meant including population planning in the overall development plan, adjusting population growth to economic growth to achieve balance and proportion between the two. State birth planning was carried out countrywide from the early 1970s. The policy of later-longer-fewer *(wanxishao)*, codified in 1973, called for later marriage, longer spacing, and fewer births. At first, urban couples could have two children and rural couples three; in 1977 a two-child rule was imposed countrywide.

After Mao's death in 1976, the new Deng Xiaoping regime rewrote the script for the nation's future, rejecting class struggle and socialist revolution in favor of rapid economic growth and entry into the global capitalist system. The party's 1978 embrace of "reform and opening up" *(gaige kaifang)* produced a radical redefinition of the problem of population. Although fertility had fallen dramatically in the 1970s (from under 6 to under 3 children per woman), the problem of population momentum meant that population growth would remain strong for years to come. Population momentum refers to the continued growth of a population after fertility falls caused by the childbearing of people already born. With rapid population growth threatening Deng's urgent agenda of quickly restoring China's greatness in the world, in 1979–1980 the demographic problem was reframed in virtually Malthusian terms as a crisis of modernization: too many people of too backward a type.[18] The population crisis framing was so powerful because it fit perfectly into the core national narrative of the People's Republic. In that narrative of nation, the Chinese Communist Party (CCP) repeatedly rescues China from disaster, putting it on the road to modernization and, for its efforts, earning the right to rule.[19] The initial solution focused on quantity restriction, drastically reducing the number of births per couple.

The CCP's dramatic Open Letter of September 1980—the document that set the party line on population for the next decade—defined the problem as one of human numbers proliferating out of control, creating a population-economy-environment crisis that was ruining China's chance of achieving the "Four Modernizations"—of agriculture, industry, science and technology, and national defense—by century's end. Undergirding this shift in framing lay a profoundly consequential alteration in discourse and underlying logic—from the Marxian discourse of state planning to the numerical discourse of modern (population) science. This shift was sanctioned by none other than Deng himself, who had declared modern science and technology the first of the four modernizations, the key to the other three. From this point on, all population policy would have to be based on "science."

A newly created science of population provided compelling numerical evidence of the severity of the problem and its (putatively) necessary solution. These new tables, charts, and figures supplied visual proof of how shamefully "backward" China's population was relative to the populations of the global powers—too large, too rapidly growing, too rural, too ill-educated, and too uneven in age structure. Of particular concern was the youth-dominated age structure. Age pyramids such as that in Figure 1 showed not a smooth progression of age groups but a bumpy pattern marked by an excess of 5–9- and 10–14-year-olds. That youthful age structure—a product of the post–Great Leap and post–Cultural Revolution baby booms— would produce a baby boom, known in Chinese as a "birth peak," from the early 1980s to the mid-1990s, distorting future social and economic development. Equally worrying was the projected rise in the absolute numbers of Chinese. Charts showing projections of future growth outlined mind-numbing prospects. Figure 2, a widely circulated chart, said that if fertility remained at three children per woman, the 1975 level, the total population would grow from 1 billion in 1980 to 4.3 billion by 2080 and then keep on

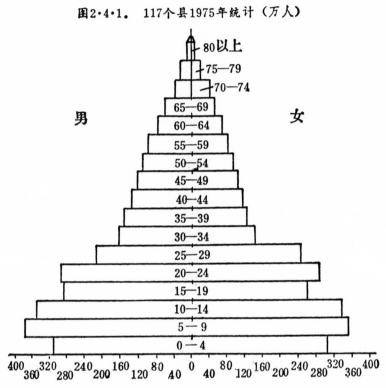

图2·4·1. 117个县1975年统计（万人）

Figure 1. "An Abnormal Age Structure That Must Be Normalized."

Note: Age pyramid shows the population by age groups in 1975 for 117 counties for which data were available. Males are shown on the left, females on the right. The figure shows an abnormally large number of people in the 5–9 age group (who were born during the Cultural Revolution) and too few people in the 15–19 group (who were born during the Great Leap Forward).

Source: Liu Zheng, Wu Cangping, and Zha Ruichuan, eds., *Population Statistics* (Beijing: People's University of China Press, 1981) (in Chinese), p. 35.

growing. Such charts provided compelling visual evidence of a frightening national future of unstoppable population growth that would eat up the gains of economic development—unless population was drastically controlled now.

Based on the research of some high-profile defense scientists, the regime declared that "the only solution" was to limit all couples to one child beginning immediately, regardless of the social costs. (The science behind that policy choice was deeply problematic; I explain how in Chapter 3.) With the nation's prosperity and the party's legitimacy as an economic modernizer at

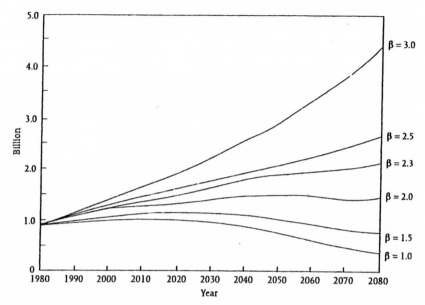

Figure 2. Projections of Future Growth under Different Fertility Assumptions.

Note: Beta = total fertility rate

Source: Song Jian and Li Guangyuan, "Quantitative Research on the Problem of Population Development," *Economic Research* 2 (1980) (in Chinese), p. 63. From Greenhalgh, *Just One Child: Science and Policy in Deng's China* (Berkeley: University of California Press, 2008).

stake, in 1980 the one-child policy was officially adopted. Population rose quickly on the political agenda. After a nationwide sterilization campaign provoked violent resistance, in 1984 the policy was quietly "perfected" to allow two children for rural couples whose first was a girl. This daughter-only *(dunuhu)* or one-and-one-half child policy was officially endorsed in 1988 and remains the party's policy today.

In the early 1990s, in response to rising fertility, an imminent birth peak, and the belief that the market was not yet strong enough to lower fertility desires, the population crisis rhetoric was forcefully revived to justify a sec-ond major crackdown on births. The May 1991 Decision of the Central Com-mittee and State Council on Stepping Up Birth Planning Work and Strictly Controlling Population Growth announced that the task of reining in popu-lation growth had not been completed, putting enormous pressure on the country's modernization efforts. Describing birth planning as a major event tied to the rise or fall of the nation, it placed the burden of quickly finishing the job squarely on the backs of party committees and governments at all levels, urging cadres to have a strong sense of responsibility to history and sense of the urgency of the times. The crisis-crackdown narrative thus persisted as the predominant formulation of the population problem throughout the Deng era (from 1979–1980 to the early 1990s), making that the darkest—and, in the West, still best known—time in China's population politics.

From the beginning, the issue of population *quantity* was linked to that of *quality*. China's people had backward bodies and backward minds, making them uncompetitive in the global economy and unfit for citizenship in a modern state. The solution was to foster superior *(yousheng)* persons, understood as global persons, who fit the highest international norms on health, education, and ethics. Initially the effort was primarily eugenic—preventing defective births through medical and legal means. Later, as the notion of quality (more generally rendered as *suzhi*) expanded to include health, education, and child rearing more generally, all social forces were encouraged to promote the rearing of high-caliber youngsters, who would grow into a high-quality labor force.

From Labor-Intensive to Human Capital–Intensive Development

Throughout the 1980s and early 1990s, a globalizing China sought to maximize economic growth at any cost based on the exploitation of cheap labor. Population governance was aimed at boosting the per capita GDP by lowering the growth of the denominator—the number of people. China's official problem of population was framed as one of economic modernization: too many Chinese of too poor a quality put intense pressure on China's economic and environmental resources, hindering the nation's development and global rise. Population governance, in short, was a matter of economic governance.

In the 1990s the labor-intensive model was beginning to reach limits. As the decade wore on, problems of social polarization, social protests, and environmental degradation were becoming more pronounced. The regime's concern to preserve "social harmony and stability"—essential to sustaining the legitimacy of the ruling Communist Party at a time of wrenching socioeconomic change and the development of Chinese capitalism—deepened. With the global shift toward a knowledge-based economy, in which knowledge is the new source of the wealth of nations and the foundation of national strength, it became clear to China's leaders that in order to sustain growth, meet the demands of a highly competitive global economy, and consolidate the global gains made so far, it was imperative that they start laying the foundations for a shift to a knowledge-based economy. China's reform leaders had already laid the groundwork for that shift in successive waves of policies aimed at supporting modern science, technology, and education. Building a new knowledge economy involved, according to World Bank advisors to the Chinese government, the formation of an institutional regime, an information infrastructure, and an innovation system supporting the creation and effective use of new knowledge.[20] It also involved strengthening the nation's human capital. Indeed, human capital—capital embodied in humans in the form of health, education, skills, talent, savvy and, most generally, the ability to create and use knowledge effectively—is the very foundation of a knowledge economy, the factor that—again according to World Bank advisors—will determine China's competitive edge.[21] The biopolitical project on population—which had been designed precisely to create a lower-quantity, higher-quality populace—was harnessed to this important new task.

In the 2000s, as China's overall reform strategy has shifted to ameliorating the social problems caused by the focus on rapid economic growth at any cost (while of course maintaining high growth rates), and to creating a higher-quality population to spur the development of a knowledge-based economy, the governance of population has shifted.[22] From largely an economic problem focused on quantity of people, population has become a social and human problem centered on the quality of China's people. Older economic concerns continue to claim attention, yet newer social problems are moving center stage. These shifts, only partly in place today, are evident in two important documents: the Eleventh Five-Year Plan for National Economic and Social Development (2006–2010) and the January 2007 party and State Council Decision on Fully Enhancing the Population and Family Planning Program and Comprehensively Addressing Population Issues (below, simply 2007 Decision).[23]

Population Governance as Social and
Human Governance (c. 2000–)

In the early 2000s (2007–2008), economic problems of population continue
to command official attention. Although China has completed the demographic transition to low fertility and mortality and now boasts fertility far
below replacement level (1.8 according to official figures, 1.5–1.6 according
to leading demographers), quantity problems—fertility, population growth,
and population size—remain prominent concerns. As the 2007 Decision
explains, population growth exhibits "unprecedented complexity" (that is, it
varies by location and group); fertility is "at realistic risk of rebounding";
three population peaks are coming (in population size, labor force, and the
aged); and population growth remains strong, with 8–10 million Chinese a
year being added.[24]

Population growth is still deemed a threat to China's economic development and global rise, but the rhetoric is now more muted: the current crisis is
potential rather than actual. As the 2007 Decision puts it, population growth
puts heavy pressure on economic development, social construction, and re-
sources/environment. These are "prominent contradictions and problems"
that must be solved for China to become an "all-inclusive well-off society."[25]
In contrast to the early 1980s, when all parts of the population were targeted
for fertility control, today the problem of excessive fertility is concentrated
among specific subgroups. Two groups are cause for particular concern: the
huge migrant population, now 140 million strong (well over 10 percent of
China's 2008 population of 1.328 billion), and the poverty population, which
is concentrated in the central and western parts of the country. Since fertility is largely, if tentatively, under control, a crackdown is no longer needed.
Rather, the solution is to "stabilize the low fertility level" by enforcing the
one-child policy for at least the next ten years.

Another economic problem is the damage that rapid population growth
inflicts on China's environment and natural resources. In 1980, population
pressure on resources/environment was a major rationale for adopting the
strict one-child policy. This emphasis continues today. Although environmental policy is the responsibility of another government agency, the Population and Birth Planning Commission (the central government agency responsible for population affairs) is charged with facilitating the coordinated

and sustainable development between population, resources, and environment, and carrying out propaganda about the role of excessive population growth in environmental deterioration.

Since the mid-1990s there has been a growing emphasis on new problems of social governance. Gaining preliminary control over the so-called fertility crisis gave population officials the political space to begin addressing the social and human costs of the intense focus during the 1980s and early 1990s on drastic population control at any cost. In the mid- to late 1990s, the primary emphasis was rural women's bodies and reproductive health, which had been badly damaged in the rushed campaigns to reach urgent population control targets. Spurred by new thinking in the international population community, which rejected target-centered approaches in favor of a new concern with women's reproductive health and rights, in the mid-1990s China began a major reorientation of its birth program. Known as the "two transformations" *(liangge zhuanbian),* that reorientation involved gradually phasing out coercive campaigns while adding an important new emphasis on women's health and quality of care to the older concern with demographic goals.[26]

Addressing the Social Dislocations Caused by Rapid Change

Under the Hu Jintao–Wen Jiabao administration (2003–present), the population problem is being reframed as one of social and even human development. Moving away from Deng's emphasis on rapid economic growth at any cost, the current regime focused first on the social dislocations caused by China's rapid entry into the global economy. Indeed, an emphasis on social justice and social governance—in particular, addressing the dire needs of disadvantaged groups through a variety of measures that "put people first" *(yiren weiben)*—has been the hallmark of the Hu–Wen regime.[27] For its part, the population field began to direct much of its energy to resolving the dire social problems caused, or worsened, by its earlier stress on pushing fertility down as fast as possible. While not addressing the human trauma and social suffering that had been imposed on China's rural people during the coercive campaigns of the 1980s and early 1990s, it did seek to lessen two major distortions in the social structure.

The first cluster of social structural problems stems from the strong sex preference exhibited by Chinese couples in a reform environment that has not been especially friendly to women. The result has been a rapid rise in the sex ratio at birth (the details can be found in Chapter 2). After remaining publicly silent for years, in a March 2000 Decision, the Central Committee and State Council finally placed this issue on the agenda of the birth establishment, instructing it to normalize the sex ratio among babies within ten years.[28] Since then, the anxiety surrounding this issue has intensified. Facing a rapid, near-term rise in the number of poor rural men unable to marry—unless things change, officials warn, by 2020 one in five young boys will be unable to marry—population officials have created a narrative of impending demographic crisis in which a large mass of potentially violent unmarried men constitutes a "social time-bomb" that is waiting to explode, disrupting the social harmony and stability of the nation.[29] The solution is to mount comprehensive efforts to address both the current problems (in particular, the widespread practice of prenatal sex determination and sex-selective abortion) and their underlying causes (the most general being the low social value accorded women and girls).

Rapid fertility decline has also accelerated the aging of China's population. (Again, the specifics are in Chapter 2.) In a context in which few enjoy public forms of social security and health insurance, and sons are becoming ever less filial, the care of the elderly has become an acute social problem, one the population establishment began seriously to address in the early 2000s. Resisting a crisis framing—so far—population officials have observed that China has crossed the threshold of an aged society and that the nation's health and welfare systems are ill equipped to serve a growing army of the elderly. The long-term solution, being addressed by several government agencies, is to gradually develop and improve the old-age security system. For its part, the population commission is "pro-actively respond[ing] to population aging" by introducing various sorts of old-age benefits to reward people who have followed state rules on childbearing and to encourage others to follow suit.[30]

Population and Reproductive Insecurity

Twenty-five years of breakneck-speed development have led to structural imbalances in China's economy and growing contradictions in its development project. In the Hu–Wen era, there has been a heightened sense of threat—from shortages of energy and raw materials, natural disasters, man-made disasters (mine explosions, for example), epidemics, and political disturbances, to name but a few—and a major governmental effort to reduce such risks to social stability and party legitimacy through the creation of new systems to anticipate, avert, and manage emergencies of every kind.[31] Responding to these larger state concerns, the population field has made the alleviation of selected population-related risks a second new governing objective in the 2000s. The Severe Acute Respiratory Syndrome (SARS) crisis in 2003, together with the growing HIV/AIDS epidemic, alarmed the population establishment, placing the issue of risks to the national body firmly on the national agenda. In response, the population minister Zhang Weiqing (service 1998–2008) introduced a new framing, "population security," explaining that "a country's overall power and national security [should] not suffer harm because of population problems."[32] The solution was to extend population work to include health work, including defending against the threats of sexually transmitted diseases (STDs) and HIV/AIDS, particularly among adolescents.

A second problem of risk, identified in 2007, is the "reproductive insecurity" faced by couples who heeded the call to have only one child, but then suffered the serious injury, disability, or even death of their single child. The one-child couple is now designated a special type of family that is "weak in resisting risks."[33] The solution is to help couples in such circumstances who have not had an additional child through birth or adoption by providing economic assistance (monthly subsidies from age 49), spiritual comfort, and care in solving life problems.[34]

A Quality Population for a Knowledge-based Economy: Health, Education, Genetics

Today, with the effort to shift from a low-cost, labor-intensive economy to a higher-cost, knowledge-intensive economy, the quality of the nation's workforce has taken on added emphasis. Despite China's enviable stock of human capital relative to the developing world, its leaders and their international advisors agree that the nation's labor force remains uncompetitive on a global scale.[35] Many of China's workers, official documents complain, are unable to meet the challenge of global competition in the new, knowledge-based economy due to the low quality of their health and low level of their education. In a contemporary framing, the unacceptable quality of the workforce is seen as detrimental to "social development and harmony," the "efficiency of resource use," and the "comprehensive competitiveness" of the Chinese nation, a phrase we return to below.[36] The solution is to further upgrade the health and education of the Chinese people, fostering indigenous talents and lifelong learners, through a combination of enhanced state investment and training of individuals to become self-enterprising, self-cultivating agents of their own lives.

In the early 2000s, a sharp rise in the number of "defective infants" has led to a renewed concern about the biological "quality" of the next generation. According to data from the nation's birth deformity monitoring center, of the 20 million babies born each year, birth defects now affect 800,000 to 1.2 million, a 40 percent increase since 2001.[37] The causes are many but include persistent poverty in some areas, growing environmental pollution, and widespread use of coal for energy (coal mining areas tend to have high levels of birth defects). The rise in birth defects not only burdens families and society at large, the official story claims, it undermines the project of creating a biologically optimal population and of improving human capital more generally. As a top population official put it, this trend "directly affects China's comprehensive national strength, its international competitiveness, [and] sustainable socioeconomic development, as well as the realization of our strategic vision to construct a full-scale well-off society."[38] The solution—now a major priority—is to proactively prevent birth defects by various means of genetic "engineering" that involve upgrading women's health services and universalizing prenatal genetic screening, counseling, and diagnosis.[39]

Promoting "Human Development" and Human Capital

Unlike the earlier problems of quantity and quality, governmental attention to these new problems is not justified solely on economic grounds. The goal of this new, more social field of population governance is to promote "human-centered development" or "all-round human development." In the regime's language, the goal is to construct an "all-inclusive harmonious socialist society" through the implementation of a "scientific concept of development" *(kexue fazhan guan).* These elusive yet multivalent terms, introduced by Hu Jintao in the early 2000s, signal broad shifts in China's strategy for reform and modernization. As Premier Wen explained in 2004, the novel approach means "economic and social development that are comprehensive, well-coordinated, and sustainable" as well as "development that has [the welfare of] human beings in mind."[40] A "scientific concept of development," an official spokesman summarized, means "human-oriented reform."[41] According to a commentator on the Eleventh Five-Year Plan, policies that adhere to a scientific concept of development are ones that "consider people's feelings, respect people's rights, [do not] ignore people's needs, and take people's freedom and all-round development as the final aim."[42] From now on, economic growth is to be only the means to the larger end of developing the human potential of the Chinese people.[43] With this new emphasis on the people at the heart of the development process, China is attempting to switch gears "from over-reliance on a cheap labor force, [limited] funds, and natural resources, to a growing dependence on a well-educated labor force, advanced science and technology, and human resources."[44] How that scientific concept of development will be concretely applied in population and birth work is just being worked out now (in late 2008 and 2009). In October 2008, the national population commission announced plans for the "in-depth study and practice" of the scientific concept of development while provinces around the country are launching pilot activities.[45]

These official explications are interesting in themselves, yet they also carry larger implications worth noting. First, with its stress on fostering the health, education, and social security of the people, and on supporting gender equity in society, the population field is actively promoting the development of China's people and the quality of China's society. Both are key elements of the "human capital" that forms the foundation of a knowledge-based economy. Second, because human capital is embodied in people themselves, its accumulation requires initiative on the part of the people. The government cannot force people to become "quality persons." It can only provide good education and health services and foster the development of the types of people who will take advantage of them. In encouraging "human development," the regime and its population officials are trying to induce people to become self-governing, self-enterprising persons who will take charge of their own lives and work to advance their own health and education, and to make learning a lifetime endeavor. Third, as projects of social and human development become increasingly important to the regime's overarching reform agenda of creating a knowledge-based economy, the administration of population can be expected to become an ever-larger part of PRC governance more generally.

Population Management as Social Systems Engineering: Hidden Logics

From this overview of how the problem has been defined in policy discourse and practice, we can see that the field of population governance has not only shifted its focus, it has also grown enormously in scope. From lowering quantity and raising quality, population governance has developed into a huge domain of social policy, the social part of the larger project of what official discourse calls the "comprehensive governance" of China's people, economy, and environment. As problems related to population have multiplied, more and more sectors of government and society have been drawn into the management and cultivation of China's people. In the area of quantity, the party and state have indeed been the major agents of population control, but they have recruited ever more sectors of government to assist. The "governors" of population quality have been more diverse. By now, they include a host of medical, educational, psychological, and other professions; the public security bureau; the pharmaceutical ministries; the party-affiliated mass associations; the economic sectors of the government; the agencies in charge of the environment and natural resources; the bureaucracies involved with social security; business corporations and, to a lesser extent, nonprofit organizations; and, of course, parents and grandparents. From a specialized activity of one division of government, population work has developed into an all-encompassing governance of China's people in which, as official documents insist, "all departments and social forces must participate."

In most third-world countries, population management means family planning. It is a relatively small, specialized sector of government, usually embedded in the health ministry. Clearly, in China, population governance is something else altogether. Instead of a small, segregated division of government, population has seen continuous domain expansion and multiplication of governors. To understand this and other distinctive features of China's project on population, we need to uncover the logics that underlie it. These logics have pervasive influence, shaping the policy on population, the design of the governing apparatus, the techniques by which population is managed and reproductive subjects are fashioned, and much more.

China's approach to population governance is guided by a unique assemblage of logics that mixes elements of Confucianism, Leninism, Maoism, and social Darwinism, among others. As the coercion account has stressed, the PRC's approach to quantity control embeds the Leninist notion of the vanguard party that, through its superior knowledge of history, as given by Marxism, is justified in using Leninist work methods to lead the masses to reproductive modernity. The approach to population governance also embeds the Maoist notion of "state guidance, mass voluntarism," which holds that, through carefully crafted propaganda and education, the people can be persuaded to alter their behavior in accord with party norms. Clearly evident, too, is the logic of socialist state planning, according to which social and economic development must be planned by the state. Underlying the quality component is the traditional Confucian notion of human educability and perfectability. Lurking behind the ambitious goals for population control and enhancement, one can find the social-Darwinist assumption of fierce competition between nations and races in the international struggle for survival. And so on.

There is yet another set of logics, an overarching one that quietly shapes much of what is said and done in the name of population in the PRC. Because we have lacked ways to think about these connections, until very recently this set of rationales has largely remained virtually invisible. This is the reasoning of modern science. More specifically, it is the logics of cybernetics and systems theory, and their practical application, systems engineering. The application of this rationale to population is both strange and significant because cybernetics is the science of control and communications in complex machine systems—not human societies. Systems theory is a method of formal analysis of objects viewed as a series of distinct but interconnected components, or "subsystems," that work together as a "system" to produce particular results. In the PRC, population is understood as a subsystem within the larger environment-economy-society system. The parts are seen as all interconnected and, ideally, working in synchronized fashion to facilitate China's modernization. Governance is a complicated systems engineering project in which, again ideally, all the parts are coordinated and managed together to ensure the optimal developmental outcome for the system as a whole. This systems logic helps us understand why, over the years, population has been connected to ever more domains of governance and why its correct management has been fundamental to the regime's most overarching goals. This underlying systems sensibility helps us unravel other puzzles as well; before getting to those, let us briefly review its history.

The Rise of Population Cybernetics and Demographic Engineering: A Brief History

Modern science and technology emerged as a central element of Chinese population policy around 1979–1980. As noted earlier, in 1978 Deng embraced science and technology as the first of the "four modernizations," the key to the other three. Modern science and technology, to be selectively borrowed from the West, were to serve as engines of the reforms and propel China onto the world stage as a global actor.

The new regime's ideas about modern science and technology were deeply influenced by Qian Xuesen, a defense scientist and the father of China's strategic defense program. Qian was superbly well connected at the highest levels of the regime. In the Mao era, Qian was a top science advisor to Mao and Premier Zhou Enlai. In the reform years, too, he remained a top advisor to the Deng regime, wielding inordinate influence on China's science culture and science policy. In his writings, Qian promoted a distinctive political ideology linking China's technological (and scientific) accomplishments to the nation's prestige and position in the world.[46] In his influential worldview, science and technology (S&T) development would be a fundamental driver of China's economic development and global rise, and scientists and engineers, including those from the military sector, would play leading roles in the government. Qian's ideas encouraged a veritable religion of science and technology—known as scientism and technicism—based on the beliefs that all aspects of the universe are knowable through science and that science is a value-neutral instrument able to reconcile traditional Chinese values with the demands of the modern world. In Qian's worldview, scientific knowledge and advanced technology were panaceas that would bring China modernity at last. All problems of reform could be solved, and could only be solved, with the spread of scientific knowledge and the application of advanced technology. With the strong personal support of Deng and other top reform leaders, modern science and technology would become the legitimating myth of China's modernizing reforms.[47] Qian's favored brand of science—which became the dominant perspective among the political and technocratic elite—was systems theory, cybernetics or control theory, and social engineering *(shehui gongcheng)*, an approach that applies technocratic organizations and techniques to perfect society itself. From the beginning of the reform era, then, human behavior and human life itself were to be treated as components of a larger social system of state-managed control. The ideal of "scientifically managing" human life itself, which ran deeper in China than perhaps in any other nation, would be fundamental to China's approach to population.[48]

The major force behind the scientization—and cyberneticization—of population politics was Song Jian, a leading defense scientist in the missile ministry—and a key protégé of Qian Xuesen. An expert in the application of control theory to problems of missile guidance, in 1979–1980, Song adapted control-theoretic techniques to the problem of population control in a series of influential articles and a coauthored book, *Population Control Theory* (published in 1982).[49] Song's work drew heavily on the research of the Club of Rome, a group of Western scientists and engineers who, in the 1960s and 1970s, advanced a global systems model in which the separate components—the economy, the environment, the population, and so on—were intimately interconnected, so that a serious problem in one threatened the others and the stability of the system as a whole.[50] In the third world, they maintained, too-rapid population growth was ruining the environment and threatening human survival. To avert system collapse, the Club insisted, it was necessary to immediately institute drastic population control. Some associated research applying control theory to population mapped out the mathematical techniques by which the "optimal" population size and policy could be determined.[51] Song ardently embraced these ideas and techniques and energetically applied them to the task of figuring out the ideal solution to China's population problems.

Drawing on the European work, in the late 1970s, Song and a handful of colleagues at the missile ministry laid out a radically new vision of population control as a giant social-systems-engineering project. In this vision, the problem of population was one of an imminent population-economy-environment crisis. Cybernetic (or control-theoretic) equations showed that the "scientific" and "only effective" way to avert it was a drastic one-child-for-all policy to be implemented immediately.[52] Given its predictable unpopularity in China's poor, rural society, this policy could be enforced only through a system of totalistic demographic engineering centered in the state. Figure 3 displays a simple version of the Song group's notion of a multilevel, multivariable structure of population administration, coordination, and control. By seizing the initiative in a rapidly changing political environment, and taking advantage of their connections to leading scientists within the regime, Song and his colleagues succeeded in outcompeting China's social scientists of population to become the leading scientific authorities on population policy—and the chief scientific architects of the winning policy proposal.[53] Despite serious problems with their one-child-for-all plan—it took no account of social, cultural, and political factors, for example—it became the top contender, gaining official endorsement in 1980.

In the 1980s, this ideal of demographic engineering caught on to become the official model for the quantitative aspect of birth work. It was enthusiastically endorsed by Premier Li Peng, another engineer (trained in hydroelectric engineering), in 1988 when, in one of his first speeches on population, he called birth planning "a comprehensive task, or even a project of system engineering."[54] Since the early 1980s, the governors of China's population have created what they call a "giant social systems engineering apparatus" that seeks to meticulously surveil, manage, and control the reproductive lives of (now) 1.3 billion Chinese. In the 1980s and 1990s, the systems engineering model guided many aspects of population work, including population planning and policy formulation, macro-program design, and cadre evaluation. Supported by a technocratic leadership increasingly made up of engineers, the systems approach to population—in which governance is conceived as a huge systems-engineering project guided by science (that is, sophisticated quantification)—has been ardently embraced by the current Hu–Wen leadership.[55] The centrality of these logics is evident in a series of large-scale research projects launched since 2003 that include population in

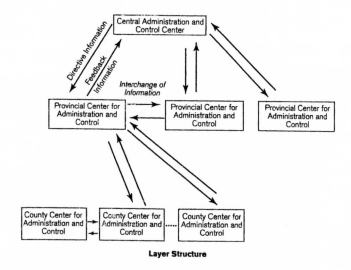

Layer Structure

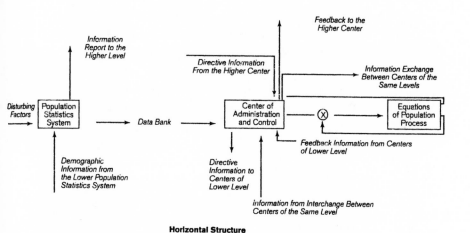

Horizontal Structure

Figure 3. A Demographic Technocracy Waiting to Be Constructed.
Model of a large population control system.

Source: Song Jian, Chi-Hsien Tuan, and Jing-Yuan Yu, *Population Control in China: Theory and Applications* (New York: Praeger, 1985), pp. 30–31. From Greenhalgh, *Just One Child: Science and Policy in Deng's China* (Berkeley: University of California Press, 2008).

multifactorial models of China's development. These include the research behind the Medium- to Long-term Science and Technology Development Plan, the Eleventh Five-Year Plan (2006–2010), and China's National Strategy for Population Development (2004–2007).[56]

The systems-engineering model has also occupied a central place in the early 2000s reforms of the population program. Under the banner of Hu Jintao's scientific development concept, the "engineers" of China's population "subsystem" (planners, officials, implementers, researchers) continue to technically refine the apparatus of governance through informatization and computerization—using advanced computer technology to gather, store, and make managerial use of data on more and more people and behaviors. Today, for example, promoting "guidance by informatization" is a major duty of the population and birth commission. This involves constructing a national database of basic demographic information, taking charge of birth planning statistics and their analysis, using data to supervise population and birth planning development, and issuing early warnings of population safety problems, among other things.[57] Despite the many gaps in the network of control, China's population governors have created a form of vital politics that, even today, is the most state-centric and techno-scientific in the world.

Of course, things are more complex than a simple story of social engineering would suggest. In recent years, other forces have been mitigating the effects of the technocratization of birth work. The rapid marketization of economic, social, and political life, combined with political and legal changes such as the growing recognition of citizen rights, including the right to freedom from official abuse, are loosening the grip of state population controllers. In response to these and other forces, the state is slowly retreating from micromanaging reproduction and actively transferring some responsibilities for managing social life to individuals. At the same time, other notions of good governance are beginning to complicate and perhaps compete with the techno-scientific ideal of a perfectly engineered society. As just noted, since the early 2000s, the state has made new notions of human governance and cultivation central to its governing strategy. In an intriguing juxtaposition of logics—one scientific, the other humanistic—the state is now attempting to advance China's national and global agendas by using a "scientific concept of development" in order to promote "all-round human development." China's leaders recognize that the quality of China's people is central to the nation's continued rise and are attempting to use advanced science and technology to improve human quality. Indeed, the very notion of a scientific concept of development is a hybrid construct that appears to include humanism at its core. What kind of "human development" can and will emerge in the state-dominated, scientistic culture of the PRC should be one of the most interesting stories of the early twenty-first century.

Why the One-Child Policy Remains in Place Today

We turn now to the puzzle at the heart of China's population politics in the twenty-first century. Why, given ultra-low fertility, rapidly rising social costs, and a shift toward human governance, do China's leaders hold fast to the one-child-with-exceptions policy? One reason, for sure, is political: after insisting for three decades that the one-child policy was economically essential, politically correct, and worth all the human sacrifice it has exacted, few of China's top leaders would dare to propose abandoning it. Another reason is leaders' fears of the social instability that might result from a policy relaxation. Such fears appear to be well grounded. In the last decade, mass demonstrations triggered by feelings of injustice have grown astronomically, in number and in size. The anguished demonstrations by parents who lost their only child in the 2008 earthquake in Sichuan suggest the intensity of the feelings that might be provoked should the one-child policy now be relaxed. (Sichuan parents who lost their only child were allowed to have another without penalty.)[58]

Yet beyond these political concerns lies another reason for the persistence of the one-child policy: the logic that lay behind the policy's adoption in 1980—the notion that population constituted a catastrophic threat to the nation's modernization and ability to become a global power—remains securely in place. Because this framing of the problem appeared scientific (it was promoted by a natural scientist and supported by a deluge of numbers and mathematical formulae) and it was politically useful to China's leaders, over the years this narrative became deeply embedded in population thinking and practice. Although today the threat is deemed *potential* rather than *actual*, the crisis narrative still underlies population policy, informing virtually all documents on the population problem. The power of the crisis narrative is such that even some of those now urging a policy change are justifying their alternative policies as responses to the nation's "crises" of low fertility, old-age support, missing females, and so on.

The doctrine of population as threat provides the reasoning behind the reaffirmation of the one-child rule in the 2007 Decision on population. The Decision describes the population situation now as "good in the overall sense," but insists that the policy on births must not change because of heavy population pressure on economic and social development and on resources/environment.[59] More specifically, in the near future China faces a series of potentially destabilizing population problems, including a low but unsteady fertility level, several imminent population peaks, persistent poor quality, and a distorted sex ratio at birth that threatens social stability. Reflecting the systems logic that everything is connected to everything, so that a change in one will cause cascading, eventually catastrophic, changes in all the others, the Decision states that "without exception, all substantial issues that China encounters in its efforts to achieve . . . development are closely related to quantity, quality, structure and distribution of the population," so that "any error committed on the population issues will exert long-term irreversible impacts on economic and social development."[60]

Behind the new policy decision lay a huge, three-year research project (2004–2007)—called China's National Strategy for Population Development—that was authorized by party general secretary Hu Jintao in 2003. The research had three major parts—"the view of scientific development," "the trend of population development," and "significant relationships between population, economy, social resources, and environment"—as well as forty-two subprojects. Three leading systems researchers—including Song Jian—were in charge of this massive effort.[61] Despite the new emphasis on human development, today the central doctrine implanted by the systems scientists—that population is a potential threat to the nation's well-being and global position that must be averted at almost any cost—remains in place. Until this rationale is effectively challenged, the one-child-with-exceptions policy is likely to remain in place.

2

Creating Global Persons
and a Global Society

Around 1980, China's party-state began to construct an elaborate social-systems apparatus designed to "engineer" the nation's rise by transforming China's backward masses into a scientifically normalized, modern society fitting of a global power. What happened when a putatively scientific policy created by an aspiring techno-scientific state was imposed on Chinese society?

The standard view of China's population politics neglects the story of science and engineering, emphasizing state coercion instead. Society figures in this account largely as an acceptor of or, more often, resister to, the one-child policy. While compelling in some ways, this account greatly underestimates the subtlety, sophistication, and adaptability of Chinese modes of statecraft. In the last chapter, I began sketching out an ethnography of the party-state and the changing projects it has pursued under the label "population." Here we see how society has been positioned in those projects—initially as target or object, and then increasingly as self-governing subject. I will argue that the birth program has worked not primarily through force, though that was important in certain times and places. The program's main mode of operation has been more positive or productive, in the sense that it has established new (supposedly) scientific norms guiding modern, global personhood, and then worked to normalize society to those standards. This perspective suggests that the program has worked not so much by oppressing people as by changing their subjectivities—their sense of self, their bodies, their desires, and their hopes for the future. The conventional state–society struggle story is not wrong but it is partial, referring only to some times and places. This newer story about the creation of new persons to facilitate China's global rise allows us to see more things, and to draw fresh conclusions about what the program accomplished, in addition to terrible social suffering. Understanding this process requires a closer look at changing modes of subject-creation.

The politics of population affords an exceptional window through which to observe the momentous transformations taking place in Chinese selfhood and society in the reform years. From research on the Maoist decades, we are familiar with the various unfree selves of high socialism, subjected to a party-state intent on leaving no domain of society outside its purview. The marketizing reforms initiated in the late 1970s and early 1980s, and deepened in the 1990s and 2000s, have spawned very different kinds of subjects that bear similarities to, yet remain in key ways different from, those of the industrialized societies of the West. In neoliberal market regimes of the advanced West, government regulation is limited and indirect. The state transfers as many responsibilities as possible to individuals and communities by instilling in them the capacity to make decisions and govern themselves responsibly. Individuals are expected to deal with the uncertainties of the market by becoming entrepreneurs of the self, autonomous actors who make decisions, follow their desires, and seek to optimize the quality of their lives.[1] Students of contemporary China have described similar kinds of self-conscious, entrepreneurial, self-optimizing, self-governing persons emerging in the globalizing market economy of the 2000s.[2] Yet the PRC is distinctive in that its gradually neoliberalizing market coexists with a still-strong state. In *Governing China's Population,* Edwin A. Winckler and I call this unusual assemblage of state and societal practices *Leninist neoliberalism,* a configuration in which Leninist logics and techniques continue to coexist with, and inform, the development of "advanced liberaltype" market principles and practices.[3] We use this term advisedly. The early Hu years saw the rise of a sharp ideological critique of "neoliberalism." In the ideological context of the PRC, political scientist Joseph Fewsmith explains, this term serves as "a vaguely defined catch-all phrase that includes not only the 'market fundamentalism' of conservative economists but also much of Western economics ... [as well as] the much derided 'Washington Consensus.'"[4] Yet even as it critiqued "neoliberalism" in theory, in practice the Hu–Wen leadership team has encouraged the use of many techniques of governance that closely resemble techniques used in the neoliberal regimes of the West. Our term Leninist neoliberalism high-lights the continued centrality of the party-state in managing the processes of marketization and de facto neoliberal governmentalization that under-gird transformations in selfhood.

Many scholars of contemporary China are now grappling with the nature of this complex formation. In their introduction to an edited collection of essays on the rise of the private Chinese self, anthropologists Aiwha Ong and Li Zhang have suggested that, in response to market forces, self-governing practices are proliferating in daily life. Although they do not ex-amine changes in the state or its governing practices, they argue that the spread of these self-governing practices is constrained by the existence of socialist state limits on behavior in certain designated domains of collective or state interest. As they put it, "neoliberal principles of private accumula-tion and self-interest . . . are not allowed to touch key areas that remain firmly under state control."[5] The picture they present is one in which the market is the main motor force behind the rise of the private self; the role of the state, which seems to resist neoliberalization ("the Chinese authorities have clearly and firmly rejected the adoption of neoliberal thinking and strategies"),[6] is to set limits on privatizing tendencies.

The field of population/reproduction is the single most striking case of an arena of social governance still tightly managed by the state. Based on close study of state and society, *Governing China's Population* shows that in this state-dominated arena of social life, self-interested, self-governing individu-als are rapidly emerging, and they are doing so not only because of the spread of market dynamics, but also because of deliberate policy choices by the state.[7] In a process that was initiated under Jiang Zemin (1993–2003) and is deepening under Hu Jintao, the state is strategically using market dynamics and neoliberal-type principles and policy instruments to its own advantage. We argue that, in seeking to retain its Leninist vanguard role, the party has opted to lead the establishment of neoliberalism in China by actively promoting instruments that shift from direct to indirect state regu-lation, devolve functions to local society, and instill attitudes of personal responsibility. As of around 2004, when the story told in *GCP* ends, vital politics remained a hybrid formation that combined Leninism and neolib-eralism in varying mixes in different subfields of population/reproductive governance. As my coauthor put it, from the regime's point of view, the making of policy remained largely Leninist; from society's view, life was becoming increasingly neoliberal.[8] What *GCP* suggests, then, is that in China there is an interpenetration of rationales such that market logics affect state practices, while state logics deeply influence market choices. A careful study of the party-state—its mentalities, governing practices, techniques of subject-creation, and so on—is thus essential to an understanding of the forms neoliberalization is taking in China today. A close study of the state is especially important because the private selves emerging today are highly differentiated, and some of that differentiation is produced by deliberate state efforts to create varied kinds of subjects needed for the success of its modernization projects. In this chapter I bring the role of the state in the creation of self-governing (reproductive) individuals into clearer focus. I chart the shifting techniques of governance by mapping out the changing methods by which the state has sought to create modern reproductive persons (or subjects). Since 2004, the trends described in *GCP* have accelerated, while taking some new twists and turns. I bring the story up to date here, highlighting the emergence of the self-fashioning, global-minded subject and the rise of a vital politics deeply infused by money.

Just as, in the Maoist era, state projects of societal transformation created new categories of persons essential to the socialist revolution (key categories included Maoist classes, agricultural and nonagricultural households, and minority nationalities), in the post-Mao years, state projects of societal modernization have been spawning new categories of persons critical to the nation's global rise. The success of the regime's project to modernize population/reproduction has hinged on the creation of three general categories of persons, or subjects: "the reproductive woman," charged with lowering the birth rate; "the quality child," the embodiment of superior body and mind; and "the good mother," tasked with nurturing that perfect child. (Fathers, because they were not the primary biological reproducers, were treated as irrelevant.) There have been many other, more specific categories as well that I will return to later.

As noted earlier, the birth-and-quality project was aimed at remaking both individuals and society as a whole. My examination of these efforts begins with the state and the scientific rationales behind its venture to create a globally competitive society standardized to the modern norms. I then sketch out several modes of individual subject-creation, working historically and distinguishing rural from urban. I identify four main modes of fashioning modern reproductive subjects in operation between 1980 and around 2008: (a) brute subjection, the mode of person-making featured in the coercion account; (b) the formation of "revolutionary-socialist subjects" through Maoist "voluntarism"; (c) the creation of "market-socialist subjects" by marketization and program reform aimed at "human-centered governance"; and (d) the making of more purely self-interested, self-governing reproductive subjects through the intensification of globalization and money politics. I then move to the aggregate level, asking how successful the regime has been in modernizing Chinese society to the global norm. In the final section, I turn to the dark underside of these overreaching efforts, showing how the state's project on population/reproduction modernization has spawned large numbers of "unmodern" persons and growing gaps between the sexes and ages. These trends not only diminish huge numbers of lives, they pose serious threats to China's further modernization and global rise.

In tracing the making of different categories of persons, I also tell a larger story about critical shifts in China's vital politics. One shift, just suggested, is from a negation of individual subjectivity through the use of direct, coercive techniques of governance to an active fostering of the self through more indirect, market-oriented techniques. Another shift is from population quantity to population quality, and, most recently, to the individual human as the central focus of population politics. A third key shift is from state-centric to multicentric governance of population. Not just the party-state, but also many other social forces, each with its own norms, have been increasingly involved in managing and perfecting China's society. Although these shifts have been underway since the 1980s, the 1990s was the pivotal period. In that decade, the party's official embrace of market socialism, the country's rapid entry into global economic and social policy circuits, and the sharp decline in fertility to below-replacement levels provided the birth program with compelling stimuli to experiment with new ways of governing China's people. Many of the key program reforms were initiated as trial pilot projects in the early to mid-1990s, extended countrywide in the late 1990s, and embraced as official doctrine of the Hu–Wen administration in the early 2000s.

State Science: New Norms for a Global Society

Under Mao, China became an arena of endless class struggle and socialist revolution. The chairman's last great adventure, the Cultural Revolution of 1966 to 1976, set worker against bourgeoisie, student against teacher, child against parent, taking the nation to the brink of ruin. By the time of Mao's death in 1976, the reputation of the party he had led for decades was in shambles. The Deng regime that came to power in 1978 sought to restore the party's legitimacy by transforming the PRC regime into a scientific modernizer that would draw on Western science and technology to lead the nation to wealth, power, and global position. The governance of population was a critical site for the construction and later expansion of this new scientific authority rooted in nature, biology, and the body.[9] Population was an optimal site for building a techno-scientific state because the central constructs involved in its management lent themselves well to definition in biological terms. The post-Mao state defined population (the quantity issue) as the biological reproduction of individual organisms aggregated into a larger collectivity. Race (the quality question), often conflated in Chinese political discourse with nation *(minzu)*, was understood as a biological entity to be eugenically improved to ensure fitness and competitiveness of the national "organism" in a social-Darwinist world of interracial and international competition. Finally, gender (the instrument of reproductive management) was defined as biological difference in reproductive structure and function, with women being "by nature" the main reproducers. The use of these biologized constructs permitted the state to represent these forces of awesome potential—and, in the post-Mao era, of fearsome threat—as impersonal processes in nature that had to be "objectively" studied and administered by the state and its techno-scientific experts "in the interests of the nation as a whole." Through the use of modern population science and reproductive technology, the party-state would take charge of these domains, creating a population of optimal size and characteristics that would both symbolize and facilitate China's status as a rising global power. Much was at stake in this ambitious project on population.

As we saw earlier, the development of a modern science of population was essential to the creation of the new policy that would lie at the heart of Deng's project on population. Borrowing from some unusual natural sciences of population, in 1979–1980, China's core problem of population was reframed as a two-part crisis of modernization: too many Chinese of too backward a type. Directing a wide range of newly emerging social, natural, and medical sciences to study population—the list includes population sociology, population economics, population and environment, population psychology, sexology, the science of reproductive health, and even birth planning-ology *(jihua shengyu xue)*—the state created new "scientific" norms on quantity and quality, and then widely disseminated them, seeking to lower the growth rate and eventually the size of the population *(shaosheng)*, while boosting its physical and mental quality *(yousheng)*.

These norms on population were linked to a larger body of societal norms specifying a proper, naturalized order for sex, gender, marriage, and family. Research on sexuality in contemporary China shows how this biologized paradigm, backed by the power and authority of medical science, has worked to make anatomy into something like social destiny. This highly conservative system of thought has stipulated two legitimate sexualities, male and female, each associated with a proper, culturally naturalized social role. To be male has meant to be strong, independent, and economically successful, while to be female has meant to be economically dependent, domestically competent, and concerned about appearance. Attached to these norms on sex, gender, and marriage were strong moral evaluations, with the proper roles deemed correct and good, and all others labeled incorrect and immoral. Supported by a party-state determined to use the arenas of sexuality and population to advance its larger ends, these ideals have been very widely promoted, putting strong pressure on individuals to adhere to the culturally dominant ways of living and leaving few, unevenly spread opportunities for the expression of sexual dissonance. Those who live according to the dominant norms have been considered natural, scientific, objective, and moral, while those who do not— unmarried mothers, the childless, and the nonheterosexual, for example— have been deemed abnormal and pathological. Of course, every society has a set of dominant norms on sexuality. But in China, the state's exceptional control of the mass media and of public discourse more generally, combined with its command of a vast array of material and symbolic rewards for compliance and penalties for noncompliance, has led to a high degree of intellectual and social conformity with these ideals and their behavioral prescriptions. Even in cosmopolitan Shanghai, ordinary people seem to largely accept gender differences in social duty as biologically based, natural, and necessary to personal happiness.[10]

From the Cadre Production of "Voluntarism" to Brute Subjection: The 1980s

The 1980s was a long time ago, but in the study of China's vital politics it is the key decade, when the one-child policy was first imposed on a society just recovering from the Cultural Revolution and tasting the first fruits of economic reform. Although the story of this first post-Mao decade is a familiar one, by mapping it out analytically and placing it alongside more current forms of reproductive politics, we can see the huge, qualitative changes that have taken place in the fashioning of reproductive subjects in contemporary China.[11]

During the long 1980s—a decade that began in 1979 and ended around 1993—the preeminent norm promoted by the state's birth planning bureaucracy was that of quantity: one child for all. Although policymaking was guided by science, policy enforcement was guided by party ways of doing things established under Mao. Under the Maoist ideal—"state guidance, mass voluntarism"—the party relied on propaganda-and-education *(xuanchuan jiaoyu)* to persuade people to change their ways, adding economic, social, and political carrots and sticks, if necessary, to back it up. The characteristic technique of enforcing party policy, including population policy, was the Maoist mobilizational campaign. The Maoist campaign involved several months of intensified yet minutely organized political work in which cadres first propagandized the masses in the new norms, then selected targets for behavioral change, and finally applied sociopolitical pressures and material disincentives until the targeted people complied. Such methods are likely to strike Western readers as eminently coercive, yet in the Chinese scheme of things they were not, because (at least theoretically) they did not entail physical force. The use of physical force—which is what the Chinese mean by "coercion and commandism" *(qiangzhi mingling)*—was off limits to the communist cadre and a serious ethical breach. Virtually every policy statement on population insisted that the policy on births be carried out without the use of force. The desired result was politically "conscientious" behavioral—and, it was hoped, subjective—change.[12] This ideologically and institutionally

produced "voluntarism" was not free choice, but in the Chinese enforcement repertoire it was the best of outcomes because it could be achieved
without the use of physical coercion. The larger aim was to produce "revolu-
tionary socialist subjects": selfless, nation-minded individuals willing to
contribute to socialist revolution and construction by following party rules
and norms, even if it meant setting aside their own personal desires.

The campaign method had been used to promote birth planning in the
1960s and 1970s, and it remained the ideal technique of enforcement in the
early reform years. The Deng state sought to instill its new norms by propa-
gating enticing images of the modern, one-child family. Targeting married,
reproductive-age women, birth planners sought first to gain contraceptive
control of their bodies, and then gradually to change their minds. Enforcers
used every means of propaganda to promote the new ideal. Figure 4, a typical image, shows a happy, well-fed toddler facing a sunny future as a result
of his quality birth and upbringing. Such cultural techniques were backed
by a panoply of economic and political rewards and penalties. Couples sign-
ing a lifetime one-child pledge were showered with material benefits, while
those who seriously breached party policy were punished by loss of job, benefits, and party membership. Just behind these "coercively persuasive" techniques lay the force of law and party authority. The 1978 Constitution declared birth planning a fundamental duty of the socialist state. In 1979 chief
birth planning official Chen Muhua announced firmly that women must
subordinate their reproductive desires to those of the state. The 1982 Constitution and Marriage Law obligated both husband and wife to practice birth
planning. In 1983 party general secretary Hu Yaobang declared birth planning and, by implication, the one-child policy, a "basic state policy" (*jiben
guoce*)—off limits to criticism and mandatory for every Chinese citizen of reproductive age. No one could miss the priority of the one-child policy in the
new party order of things.

Creating "Revolutionary Socialist Subjects": Urban Quantity Control

During the 1980s, because of differences in the role of children in the family and varying enforcement environments, the politics of numbers came
to take different forms in China's cities and villages. In the cities, where

Figure 4. The Modern Family: One-Child Propaganda Poster.

Source: Stefan R. Landsberger, *Chinese Propaganda Posters: From Revolution to Modernization* (Armonk, NY: M.E. Sharpe, 1995).

children were costly to raise and added little to family economic well-being, fertility preferences were low. Although most urban residents considered the two-child family the ideal, few could afford to raise more than one. In the cities, son preference was weak. Some couples even preferred daughters, who were believed to be emotionally closer to their parents and thus more likely to provide personal care in old age. These fertility preferences greatly eased the task of enforcing the one-child policy in the cities. The government's economic incentives and disincentives made the decision to stop at one economically sensible.[13]

The political climate also fostered compliance with the new policy. Interviews with Shanghai residents suggest that in the immediate aftermath of the Cultural Revolution, the public's mind-set was submission to government dictates. Questioning official policy was equivalent to challenging the party, which could lead to imprisonment and worse. In the early years of the one-child policy, fears of political sanction acted as a powerful deterrent to would-be violators.[14]

The tight networks of control through which the regime managed the urban population also eased enforcement of the new one-child rule. The workplace *(danwei)* system that structured urban life made couples profoundly dependent on their employers, who were the source not only of jobs, but also of housing, health care, old-age support, and other necessities of life. In this setup, opposition to the one-child policy became unthinkable, for violation of the policy would bring loss of job and everything that came with it. These mechanisms of social control enabled urban birth workers to enforce the one-child policy through institutionally and ideologically produced "voluntarism."

Tight institutional controls allowed birth cadres in the workplace and neighborhood to create female bodies highly disciplined according to the state's contraceptive and fertility norms. At their workplaces, women were subject to close monitoring and management of their reproductive affairs, with everything from their monthly periods to their premarital health, marital status, contraceptive practices, and pregnancies subject to close surveillance and mandatory oversight. Supplementing workplace control was the ongoing surveillance achieved by the residential neighborhood, where voluntary enforcers of party policy kept an eye out for unorthodox behavior. Women might lodge symbolic protests against the relentless control—by refusing to fill out the proper form, for example, or skipping a mandated gynecological exam, or even manufacturing a physiological excuse for not using an intra-uterine device. But there were few avenues for real escape.

Despite the popular desire for two children, in-depth research suggests that women in China's cities gradually came to the politically "conscientious acceptance" *(zijue jieshou)* of the one-child family. Their acquiescence arose in part from their acceptance of the official line, propagated intensely by images such as the chart in Figure 2, that China faced a crisis of human numbers that necessitated a policy of one child for all. Memories of mass starvation during the Great Leap Forward remained vivid, making the government's one-child rule seem an obvious and wise response to the nation's problem of excessive population growth. Individual women felt they must voluntarily submit to "the requirement of the nation" because the needs of the nation overrode their own and because they had a civic duty as "advanced" citizens to sacrifice for the national good. Despite the deep intrusions birth cadres made in their bodies and lives, women did not find the interventions offensive because they felt that the cadres were only doing their jobs, and sensed they were exercising control in "concerned" *(guanxin)* and "caring" *(zhaogu)* ways that recognized women's own needs. In a classic example of politically produced "voluntarism," the women felt that their cooperation with the onerous demands of the birth cadres was quite freely given.[15]

Brute Subjection: Rural Quantity Control

In the early 1980s, the rural areas were home to about 80 percent of China's people. To China's leaders, it was here that the real population problem lay. The peasant family's strong need for children, coupled with the weakening of village enforcement institutions, led to intense opposition to the one-child rule from ordinary peasants and local officials alike. In that context, policy enforcers had little choice but to resort to coercive campaigns, the state's least-favored means of enforcement, to suppress dissent and gain compliance. The result can only be described as brute subjection of the masses to the will of the party-state. This manner of enforcement is specific to the rural context in the long 1980s, yet in popular and even academic discourse it has come to stand for the one-child policy. I can only summarize the process here.[16]

In the 1980s, Chinese villagers maintained strong desires for two children and lingering preferences for three. Gender was as important as number: one had to be a son. The Shaanxi villages where I worked in 1988 and 1993 were typical of nationwide patterns. Sons were needed for labor and old-age support. Daughters were valued as helpers on the family plot and caregivers in old age. These concrete benefits of children were increasingly offset by rapidly rising costs—not only of food, clothing, schooling, and health care, but also of weddings and houses for married sons. The villagers I worked with ridiculed the old idea that "many children bring much wealth" *(duozi duofu),* insisting that children were now heavy burdens *(fudan zhong).* As the 1980s wore on, desires for three children weakened, giving way to a virtually universal preference for two children—a son and a daughter. Much was at stake in ending up with one child of each gender. In the absence of publicly provided old-age support and in a fast-changing environment, children were the vital, indeed, irreplaceable keys to the economic security and survival of the family. The state's (putatively) scientific policy specifying one for all had treated social and cultural forces as irrelevant, setting the stage for a clash between the scientific norm of the state and the community reproductive norms of Chinese villagers.

Falling back on tried-and-true methods, local cadres enforced the new birth policy almost exclusively by mobilizational campaigns. In the early 1980s, couples took advantage of the new openings in the reformed political economy to fiercely resist state demands. Resistance took a huge variety of forms—from concealing pregnancies to hiding from cadres, running away to neighboring villages, and many more, all vividly described in the literature. The state responded with brutal crackdowns. In 1983 it launched a nationwide sterilization campaign, directing local officials to sterilize one member of all couples with two or more children, insert an IUD in all women with one child, and abort all unauthorized pregnancies. Birth officials sought to enforce these rules through propaganda and education, but ended up using sociopolitical pressure and, where that did not work, physical force. In this campaign, which went on for many, many months, the party violated its own rule against using physical force against the people, relying on late-term abortions, confiscation of property, demolition of houses, and other over-the-top methods that drove people in some places to violent extremes. In Shaanxi, local campaign documents described these

abusive methods used against the noncompliant in astonishing detail, sug-
gesting their authorization by upper levels of the system. The campaigns led
to heartrending forms of violence against baby girls by couples desperate for
a son. This was not subject-creation, it was the subjection of women to the
will of an unbending party, a heavy-handed suppression of women's humanity in which their bodies were forcefully controlled, even if their minds
were not persuaded.

Facing serious unrest in the countryside, from early 1984 the party
backed off for a few years. That was the time of my first fieldwork in the
Shaanxi villages, and I was amazed at the relaxed atmosphere surrounding
the population issue. The easing of pressure from the top created room for
local cadres to negotiate informal reproductive rules with the villagers—
"local policies" *(tu zhengce)*—that took account of pervasive desires for a
son. Massive resistance in the early 1980s, followed by such local negotiations carried out in villages across the country, had one positive effect. In 1984
the party softened the birth policy to allow rural couples with "only" a girl
to have another child.

Unfortunately, fertility began to rise in the mid-1980s, re-igniting the
earlier debate on how to stanch population growth. In 1991 the party responded with another harsh countrywide crackdown. This one was centered
on eliminating local policies and enforcing the 1.5-child policy nationwide.
The campaign was directed primarily at party and government officials at
all subnational levels. New rules tightened the penalties for failure and introduced a new "one-vote veto" *(yipiao foujue)* system in which cadres' overall job performance would be rated poor, with all the attending damage to
bonuses, promotions, and other benefits, should they fail to meet their population targets. Facing possible loss of their jobs, local cadres reacted in the
way the state had hoped—by overriding people's preferences and strictly
enforcing the policy. The campaigns of the early 1990s produced terror and
trauma in the countryside. In locations where fertility preferences had already fallen, the campaigns led to tense relations between party and people.
In places where desires for several children remained strong, the campaigns
resulted in violent struggle that tore communities apart. Almost everywhere, it seems, the rough methods posed threats to women's health. The
top national birth official charged with ensuring achievement of targets
told me of women being operated on while lying on the ground, with no

blankets or even anesthesia.[17] The campaigns of the early 1990s marked the beginning of the end of the era of strong-armed state imposition of its norms on rural society. For some combination of reasons—forced fertility reduction, doctoring of the numbers, and/or genuine change in people's desires—by 1993 measured fertility had fallen to about 1.8, well below replacement fertility of 2.2. Program leaders, victorious in the battle over numbers, turned to correcting some of the problems their harsh methods had caused.

Creating Market-Socialist Subjects: Rural Birth Work in the 1990s and Early 2000s

The 1990s ushered in a new era in the rural politics of population numbers, one that is still unfolding today. Although the policy on births remains essentially unchanged, the growing marketization of rural family life, coupled with "human-centered" reforms in the birth program, are fostering the emergence of more calculating, self-governing "market-socialist subjects" increasingly regulating their own reproduction in accord with state and market norms.

A Marketization of Family Size Preferences

Survey and ethnographic data suggest that by the early 2000s, the rural family-size ideal had dropped to under two. By all accounts, there has been a real decline in family size preferences in all but the poorest areas. There is also a growing willingness to end up with "only" a girl. Indeed, in some places daughters are now preferred to sons and are being actively groomed to become the primary supporters of their parents in old age.[18] Behind these changes in reproductive culture lay decades of insistent state propaganda and practice. Just as transformative, however, were the profound changes in family life brought about by China's deepening marketization and spreading consumer culture. To China's villagers, the issue that loomed largest was the escalating costs of children. In addition to schooling, health care, food, and other basics, the costs of child rearing included a new category of incidental expenses defined as essential to ensuring the bodily and mental quality of the young: nutritional supplements, educational toys, piano lessons, and more. At the same time, the economic and emotional advantages of having several were shrinking. For parents, the most frightening concern was the growing unwillingness of sons to honor their most fundamental obligation: to support their parents in old age. In the late 1980s, parents in my Shaanxi villages were humiliated when their two or three sons fought over who would have to live with them. Twenty years later, some sons are abandoning their parents altogether—with sometimes devastating effects.[19]

After more than a decade of sometimes violent struggle, the period of socialist marketization that began around 1993–1994 has seen a remarkable, though still partial, convergence in family ideals, in which villagers, especially in the more developed areas, have begun to embrace the official one-to-two-child norm as their own. Unfortunately, the lowering of rural fertility desires has been contingent on farm couples' ability to control the gender of the one or two children they bear and raise. Given an unbending and tightly enforced policy on births, couples in many areas have turned to prenatal sex determination and sex-selective abortion to ensure that they end up with a son. In many parts of the country, abortion of female fetuses is simply part of the everyday culture of family formation.[20] Although such practices solve the problems of son-obsessed couples and control-obsessed birth planners, they have fearful consequences for girls and women and for society as a whole. We turn to these in a moment.

Program Reforms: The Rise of "Human-Centered" Governance

The mid- to late 1990s also brought the initiation of major reforms in the state's birth program.[21] The achievement of ultra-low fertility gave program officials the opportunity to begin eliminating the ugliest features of the program and reorienting it in line with new international ideals of reproductive health and good governance more generally. In the 1990s, as Chinese society grew more market-minded, rights-oriented, and intolerant of administrative abuse, radical reform of the birth program became all but necessary.

From the mid-1990s the birth establishment began to phase out coercive campaigns and the abusive practices that came with them. A revealing document created in the early 1990s listed the "seven don'ts" (qige bujun) in local birth planning work. Local birth planning officials were not permitted to: arrest or harm violators or their family members; destroy property;

impound property without due process; add fees and levy fines at will; detain
noncompliers' associates or retaliate against complainers; refuse permission
for a legal birth in order to meet population plans; and organize pregnancy
checks of unmarried women. Although these officially proscribed practices
were identified in 1991, it was only in 1995 that this list was circulated
among enforcers nationwide. After that, they were gradually incorporated
into the criteria for evaluating cadre performance in most areas.[22] Although
local officials in some places managed to evade the new rules and use these
tried-and-true techniques for gaining compliance in difficult cases, by the
end of the decade, the State Birth Planning Commission, the agency in
charge of population work, had moved decisively away from the hard, mobilizational methods that had formed the core of birth planning since the
1970s. In their place it introduced a range of more client-centered, human-
oriented reforms.

The initial emphasis was on women's reproductive health, which in the
rural areas had been badly neglected in the urgent quest to achieve tight
population control targets. Influenced by the UN's 1994 Cairo Conference
on Population and Development, which adopted women's reproductive
health and rights as the new focus for international population policy,
China's leaders began actively reorienting the Chinese program to address
issues of reproductive health and quality of health care, in addition to the
traditional concerns with demographic control. Under the banners of
"client-centered reform," "client satisfaction," "quality of care," "informed
choice," and "taking people as primary," the national birth commission
launched experiments in the mid-1990s, and began institutionalizing the
changes in the late 1990s.[23]

Since then, these efforts at humanistic management in population work
have broadened far beyond the original health emphasis. Beginning in the
late 1990s, but especially since the early 2000s, the birth planning commission has introduced a series of mechanisms that it describes as "human-
oriented" and "people-friendly." All attempt to stabilize low fertility, "comprehensively solve China's population problems," and promote "all-round
human development" with a radically new approach to governance.[24] The
older approach too often relied on administrative orders, neglected the human target of governance, and supplied poor-quality products and services. Encouraged by the Hu–Wen administration, which has developed a

distinctive "pro-people" style of governing, the new approach is human-centered in that it places the human object of population governance center stage, at once attending to people's needs and fostering their capacities for self-governance. It is also deemed humanistic because of its emphasis on solving people's social and livelihood problems through economic or benefit-oriented (rather than administrative) mechanisms; and its stress on a service (rather than commandist) orientation. With these shifts in concrete techniques of governance, the state hopes to improve the quality of public management and public services and, in turn, solve the nation's population problems.[25] These new directions, which shift the accent in China's Leninist neoliberal approach toward the neoliberal end of governance, are illustrated by three mechanisms being emphasized today.

First, the population establishment is promoting a package of benefit-oriented mechanisms that includes (a) a system of incentives and old-age assistance for older rural couples with only one child or two daughters; (b) a "fewer children equals faster prosperity" program that helps families practicing birth planning emerge from poverty; and (c) a "special assistance system for couples practicing birth planning" whose single child has been injured, disabled, or died. These programs are designed to address the concrete needs that underlie high fertility preferences (for labor and old-age support, for example) and to alleviate the very real risks faced by couples who have complied with the state's minimalist birth policy. The hope is that by solving the problems of couples who currently have one child, the measures will persuade others to stop at one child as well.[26]

A second type of "people-friendly" technique emphasizes service-oriented modes of delivering contraceptive and other reproductive and child health services. Called "humanistic care," these wed "scientific management" (professionalization of personnel, gathering of detailed demographic and health assessment data, research on population development strategy, and so forth) to health care practices that attend closely to women's and children's health needs.[27]

Third is a strengthened emphasis on rule of law rather than rule by administrative fiat or party dictate. Governing through law—known in Chinese as "birth planning administration by law"—entails enforcing the official laws and regulations on births; practicing "open governance"; ensuring that people's legitimate rights and interests are respected; further developing the legal system for population and birth planning; and building grass-roots democracy by encouraging local elections of birth cadres.[28]

These reforms in the birth-and-quality project are part of a larger shift in the party's governance strategy toward "people-centered governance" *(wei-min zhizheng)* aimed at the construction of a "harmonious society" *(hexie shehui)*. A signature theme of the Hu–Wen administration, the notion of "harmonious society" is meant to shift the emphasis from an obsession with GDP growth at any cost to a more balanced development agenda that addresses the social and environmental consequences of China's rapid economic growth, including the vast gaps that have emerged between the haves and have-nots. In a major upending of party priorities, the current administration has elevated social development—including social well-being, "humanistic values," and environmental protection—to the same level as economic growth in the party's overall agenda.[29] People-centered governance seeks to reposition people away from being mere instruments of policy implementation to being more active, self-determined participants in new modes of social governance still steered by the CCP. Intended to enhance the efficiency and effectiveness of the state administration of society, these techniques involve a shift in the state's role from micro- to macromanagement. All adhere to the basic neoliberal principles of relying on the market, working through people's desires, and an offloading of responsibilities once handled by the government (especially social welfare and health care) onto society and self-governing individuals. Since the mid-1990s, population has been an important arena for the incubation of these new governmental ideas. Precisely because bad governance was so pronounced in that arena, population may have been especially important in the development of human-centered techniques.[30] Now being used in selected policy domains—most notably the building of urban communities *(shequ)*—these reforms in governing technique are being carried out in the context of broader efforts by the regime to conform to internationally accepted, essentially neoliberal, norms of domestic good governance.[31]

Solidifying the shift in approach, the birth program has launched a major "clean-up" and "humanization" of its propaganda. In mid-2007, the population commission banned the use of the crude, strongly worded sorts of messages that had been associated with rural birth control since the early 1980s. Deemed most offensive were harsh, commandist slogans such as "Spread single childbearing, control second births, prohibit third births," which was introduced during the 1983 sterilization campaign. Such strident language, the commission acknowledged, created the impression that the government was forcing people to limit their fertility. Such language stoked public resentment, officials explained, causing misunderstanding of the policy and even tarnishing the government's image.[32] In its place, local officials were instructed to choose from a selection of new, more friendly messages, such as: "The modern earth is too tired to sustain more children," or "Both boys and girls are parents' hearts." These more "civilized" and "human-oriented" slogans are meant to support the new program initiatives by creating more favorable attitudes toward the government and its policies on population.[33]

These reforms in the birth program have ushered in a new mode of creating reproductive subjects, now only partially in place. This change is signaled by a shift from what the program calls "birth according to plan" to "birth according to law." Under "birth according to plan," the regime sought direct control of every aspect of reproduction. This was subjection, and it produced more costs than benefits. By contrast, "birth according to law" seeks a more indirect form of control that works through individual desires and interests. "Birth according to law" assumes a "self-regulating individual." The social-systems apparatus that I outlined earlier is being reengineered to produce that more active kind of subject who can "autonomously" regulate herself—in the way the state wishes. With this, a critical shift is underway from individual subjection to individual *subject-ification,* which works through individual desires for such things as good health, citizen rights, individual choice, and small, modern families.

These transformations in techniques of governance have been guided by another, also partial shift, in which *social* scientific reasonings are coming to matter more. In the 1980s and early 1990s, Leninist birth planners had tried to operate the population program on a natural science model, reducing people to biological targets of control and neglecting the cultural and social dynamics of family life. The result was a human and political catastrophe. Since the early to mid-1990s, program leaders have come to believe that, to be effective, intervention must be indirect and must treat its objects as cultural subjects. The new people-centered approaches are informed in part by social-scientific understandings of reproduction in social and cultural context. Social scientists have been actively involved in the debates over program reform and policy change. I say more about their involvement and influence later.

Of course, there are limits on these trends toward humanization of population and birth work. These are highlighted by the 2001 Population and Birth Planning Law, which continues to advocate one child for all with some exceptions. Reflecting the continued sensitivity of the population question, the 2001 Population and Birth Law was created with very little public participation and remains very conservative, treating law as a tool of administration and social engineering rather than civil law. The contrast is with the 2001 revision of the Marriage Law, which was accompanied by vigorous public debate and in some respects reflects the general drift in China today toward greater individuality and autonomy in decision making.[34]

China's population planners certainly deserve credit for fostering these promising changes in the birth program, but to what extent have these reforms initiated by the Center been implemented in localities around the country? Because local birth cadres are evaluated in part on the basis of their adherence to provincial and municipal guidelines, the regime does gather data on the use of many of the concrete techniques discussed earlier: benefit-oriented mechanisms, data-based management, compliance with legal limits on births, and so on. The overall picture is one of gradually spreading use of these more people-affirming techniques, with birth cadres in the richer areas complying more and those in the poorer areas complying less. On the more intangible aspects of people-centered governance—service orientation and promotion of "humanistic values," for example—it is harder to say how much the new directions have changed things on the ground. Moreover, virtually all the data are gathered by the birth planning sector of the government; in the absence of more than a handful of independent field studies conducted since 2003, it is hard to render an independent assessment. Evidence from the very early 2000s suggests, though, that in part because of falling reproductive desires and in part because of these people-centered changes in the birth program, in many villages real changes are underway. Especially in more developed areas of the country, researchers and journalists report, the planning of small, high-quality families is becoming more truly voluntary, shaped by people's own desires as much as by the demands of the birth program.[35]

Producing the "Quality" Singleton

From the outset, the state's quantity project was closely linked to another project to ensure the "quality" of coming generations. The eugenics campaign—*yousheng youyu*, literally superior birth and child rearing—incorporated genetic engineering, but it was much broader than that, reflecting the view that humans are shaped by a broad array of genetic, environmental, and educational factors, most of which can be nurtured so that human potential can be molded to meet the nation's needs. For the state, promoting child quality—primarily genetic makeup, health, and education—justified its claim to be a scientific modernizer capable of transforming China's backward masses into a modern labor force equipped to compete in the global marketplace and a modern citizenry ready to handle the responsibilities of contemporary life.

The child quality project developed earlier in the urban areas than in the rural areas. One reason for the obsession with creating perfect children was the growing desire for only one child among city couples: with but one, that one had to be perfect. During the 1990s, the great majority of urban women came to deem one child the ideal; most expressed no preference for a son or daughter. Spurred by the rapid growth of child-enhancing resources, in the cities investments in the bodies and minds of the young began to rise rapidly in the 1980s before exploding in the 1990s, when China's consumer economy took off and the project to create the perfect child became a fixation of parents and the wider society alike.

Based on expenditures on the two projects by state and society, since around the mid-1990s, quality appears to be replacing quantity as the primary domain of Chinese population politics. The growing importance of quality is transforming the field of vital politics in several ways. First, the promotion of quality has given rise to two newly defined or configured objects of control, and thus two new reproductive subjects: "the quality child" and "the good mother," who fosters that child. Second, the creation of quality youngsters relies less on direct, coercive techniques (though those are used in genetic enhancement) than on indirect techniques that work through parental (and child) desires. Like parents elsewhere, Chinese parents have been enthusiastically embracing the official ideals of child health and education, and correcting their youngsters to these norms. The growing emphasis on quality, then, has brought greater use of positive, self-fostering techniques of governance and, in turn, the emergence of more self-interested, self-governing subjects. A third major shift is a broadening of the "governors" of population, from the state and its experts, which until recently have been the sole authority on population quantity, to a much wider array of social and market forces. Here I can only illustrate some of these trends, focusing on urban developments.[36]

Creating the "Good Mother"

A broad set of forces worked to make the quality project a woman's responsibility. These forces created a newly salient subject, the "good mother," and defined her as a mother who would sacrifice her own interests for her youngster and follow the prescriptions of the latest science in conceiving, giving birth to, and rearing a high-quality child.[37] The birth program played a major role in promoting maternal and early child health by legally preventing marriage among those deemed genetically "unfit," providing mandatory premarital, prenatal, and postnatal health checks for women, and energetically propagandizing the benefits of healthy, scientific pregnancy and childbirth.

The campaign for population quality gained great momentum in the mid-1980s, when efforts to ensure quality births were extended to include the health and education of single children. In mandatory parenting classes, and in propaganda and education disseminated through the mass media, the birth program taught mothers scientific methods for improving the child's body (through better dietary, sanitary, and illness-prevention practices, for example) and enhancing its mental capabilities, with the intent of developing the child into an able-bodied, well-educated talent for the nation. These efforts were supported by a mushrooming popular literature coaching parents in strategies for the nurturing of superior children. Popular books on fetal education *(taijiao)* and eugenic births depicted pregnancy and infant care as difficult tasks that could be successfully accomplished only with the help of medical experts and the charts, diagrams, and lists of standards offered in their pages.[38] Figure 5, published in a 1999 guidebook called *Eugenic Births and Fetal Education Work (Yousheng: Tai-jiao gongcheng),* illustrates these pedagogical efforts. The chart in Panel A

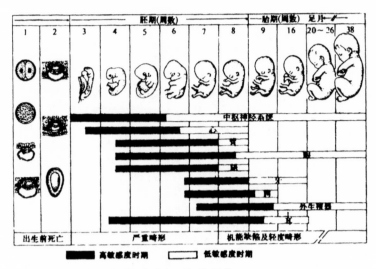

Figure 5. Ensuring a Superior Birth: Scientific Guidelines
Panel A: The Sensitivity of Various Organ Systems to Abnormality During Human
Embryonic Development.
Note: The chart shows embryonic development by weeks. The organ systems shown include heart,
eyes, teeth, and ears.

shows the sensitivity of different fetal organ systems to abnormality at different phases of the pregnancy. The diagrams in Panel B show activities that pregnant women should avoid to ensure that such abnormalities do not plague their pregnancy. The cover illustration (not shown) depicts a broadly smiling thirty-something Caucasian couple and a bouncy blond, blue-eyed baby boy. The implication is that Chinese couples, by following the guidelines in the manual, can produce babies that match the supposedly high eugenic level of white Western babies.

Women's magazines, television programs, and other media reinforced the message. The demands did not stop at infancy. Books on parenting the perfect toddler and then teenager defined child rearing as a scientific enterprise of great moment, not only for the child and his or her family, but also for the nation as a whole. Warning concerned parents to listen only to the experts— child psychologists, pediatricians, teachers, and so forth—the pedagogical materials sorted child intelligence into a series of specific abilities, listed games and exercises that encouraged the development of each, and laid out developmental milestones that parents could use to figure out where their

Panel B: Activities Pregnant Women Should Avoid.
Source: Liu Longyan and Zhang Jianhua, eds., *Quality (or Eugenic) Births and Fetal Education Work* (Beijing: China Population Press, 1999) (in Chinese), pp. 53 and 153.

child ranked on the ladder from "backward" to "prodigy." Where parental skills fell short, extra tutoring and classes were culturally mandated.

Despite the demands of this new, time-intensive form of mothering, and a Mao-era history of close identification with work outside the home, many women viewed their own sacrifice for their child as natural and necessary. Most seemed to readily accept their new roles, even if it meant giving up their own career ambitions. For mothers in the 1980s, whose educations and job opportunities had been cut short by the Cultural Revolution, a major motivation was to ensure that their children, especially their daughters, did not suffer the deprivations they had endured. Throughout the post-Mao decades, women also invested heavily in their children to ensure their own support in old age. Institutional changes ushered in by the reforms actually reinforced the importance of family support for the elderly. Moreover, with only one child, it became an urgent matter to ensure that that child would be willing to honor his or her filial obligations. Mothers dealt with these heightened anxieties by devoting ever more time, money, and energy to their only children. There are many stories of young mothers paying for pianos and piano lessons for their son or daughter, not because they expected to produce a great musician, but because they hoped the child would reciprocate with support and care later on.

Cultivating the "Quality Child"

The goal of these efforts was the "quality child," the personification and guarantor of a new and prosperous future—for parents and country alike. Beginning in the 1980s, the birth program energetically promoted child health and education, thoroughly integrating the quality project into its much better- known quantity project. The birth establishment fostered child quality by providing educational and health benefits for single children, using its vast propaganda machine to popularize an appealing image of the healthy, well-educated child, and working closely with the educational and health bureaucracies to promote top-flight health and schooling for single children. The 1980s brought a major expansion of government agencies and research institutions involved in child health and schooling. Tapping the resources of the Chinese Academy of Preventive Medicine, the Ministry of Health undertook large-scale efforts to boost child health and nutrition. These culminated in a major Program for Chinese Children's Development in the 1990s. Other state agencies oversaw the creation of a children's food industry, the formulation of laws protecting children's health, and other measures to ensure the physical well-being of the young. In the 1980s and 1990s child health became a major government enterprise. The same is true of education.[39]

Other entities and social forces, some with partly competing notions of "quality," soon took over some of the work of nurturing that exemplary child. With only one child and grandchild, parents and grandparents began to spend heavily on their "little emperors and empresses," buying for them as many health- and education-related foods, toys, lessons, and outings as possible, in an effort to guarantee their career and life successes in the increasingly competitive environment of a globalizing China. Such investments have been nourished by success stories such as that told by the 2001 best seller, *Harvard Girl Liu Ying*, whose parents started at the time of their daughter's birth to "scientifically" prepare her to get into and succeed at Harvard. The object of all these hopes and investments, Chinese youngsters have led highly structured, parent-directed lives, with little time for free play.

In the 1990s, market forces became heavily involved in creating quality children. Unlike the state programs for child health and education, corporations have worked indirectly, through shaping individual desires. Transnational corporations have been highly successful in fostering the notions that selfhood is created through consumption, and that Chinese citizens can acquire the patina of a "global person" through the consumption of their foreign goods and services. My visits to children's stores in recent years reveal that food and pharmaceutical companies have introduced a huge array of infant and toddler products, all—according to the ads—necessary for nurturing the "world-quality" child. By associating their food and restaurant experiences with science, modernity, and Western-ness, corporations such as McDonald's and Kentucky Fried Chicken have become some of the biggest promoters—and sellers—of "child quality."[40] McDonald's has marketed its meals as scientifically formulated and nutritionally beneficial, while offering special events (like talent competitions) to entertain and educate the young diners. Parents have responded positively, seeing visits to McDonald's as opportunities to nurture the bodies and minds of their youngsters, while giving them a chance to experience firsthand global, especially American, culture. By the turn of the millennium, the market and its logics of consumer desire had become major forces in the politics of population quality.

As parents have indulged their children, allowing them to make consumer decisions on snacks, toys, and even appliances for the home, there has been another shift in decision making: toward the younger generation themselves. Impressed by the ads of transnational firms, children are opting for items with global cachet, becoming consumerist versions of the global citizens the state has long tried to create. Market forces have thus worked in tandem with the state's bureaucratic efforts and societal dynamics to produce a new kind of healthy, well-educated, independent, market-minded "quality" person who will increasingly make up the citizenry of twenty-first-century China. The result is a kind of self-interested, "self-regulating" subject whose desires, preferences, and interests align with those of a gradually neoliberalizing market and state that have largely shaped those desires, preferences, and interests to their own ends.

The Emergence of the Self-Determining Subject?
The One-Child Generation Grows Up

Around 2005, this first generation of single children began reaching marriage and childbearing age. What kind of reproductive subjects will they be? What kind of parents will these young people, widely considered self-centered, uncooperative, and unable to care for themselves or others, become? It is too soon to say, but early evidence from Shanghai and Dalian suggests that this new generation of (mostly) urban singletons will manage their sexual and family lives differently from previous generations. While young people now accept the one-child policy without question, growing numbers are considering forgoing parenthood altogether. In one study of teenagers in Dalian, 18 percent of girls expressed no interest in marrying, while 32 percent said they did not want children. (In the same study, 10 percent of boys did not want to marry, while 16 percent did not want children.)[41]

A major reason is that family ties impose heavy responsibilities on women, and young women are intent on living their lives on their own terms rather than on terms imposed by others, whether that other is the state or their own parents. In the cosmopolitan areas of urban China, one thus sees the emergence of an increasingly self-interested, self-motivated, self-governing reproductive self. Indeed, in a textbook case of the rise of the private reproductive self, this is the very identity these young people are embracing. Urban young women today see their interests as different from the national interests. As some young Shanghai residents put it, "The [one-child] policy is not necessary for us. We can make our own decisions based on our education";

or: "Individually, we think and act for ourselves"; or: "The people in Shanghai are self-motivated and educated . . . so it is possible to get rid of the policy here."[42] While accepting the sacrifices their mothers made on their behalf, they are unwilling to give up their own career aspirations to have children, who are seen as impediments to the achievement of individual success. Acting as entrepreneurs of the self, they are defining their identities in opposition to those of their own mothers, and prioritizing the personal goals of individual development and career advance over motherhood. As one put it, "Even when I have children, I still want my own life."[43] Women who do want a child expect their husbands to help them raise it, a dream that may collide with reality when the time comes.

Of course, these assertions of self-control do not mean that young women in China's cities today are free of state restraints or influences. Their self-chosen desires are influenced by the larger culture of reproduction, and the state has worked for many years to structure that culture along lines consistent with its minimally reproductive policy. Yet things are changing. Young women are increasingly acting for themselves, not others; they are claiming ownership of their ideas and behavior, and they are acting entrepreneurially to advance their personal and career goals. Young people born under the one-child policy are also becoming more independent-minded about broader issues bearing on their lives and well-being. For example, the copious definition of "quality," which by the 2000s encompasses physical, educational, cultural, ethical, and political virtue, has provoked heated debates about who does and does not possess high quality. To avoid the stigma of being labeled "low in quality," those at risk are claiming that their special strengths in one area—their educational credentials, unique talents, patriotism, or upright morals, for example—ensure their high quality overall.[44] Such evidence suggests that a big shift in subjectivity is taking place, one with important implications for the state's project on population and for the kind of Chinese emerging on the world stage.

Vital Politics in the 2000s: The Triumph of Money

As the first decade of the 2000s draws to a close, the deepening of marketization and consumerism is fostering new modes of reproductive subject-making and new kinds of global Chinese persons. Two trends can be discerned. First,

China's people are becoming more globally savvy and ambitious, self-consciously making use of the resources of the outside world to produce globally superior children. In family formation as in other domains of life, there is a growing tendency for Chinese to see themselves as acting and competing not just on the national stage, but on the world stage. Second, increasingly, money speaks louder than state policy, allowing those with the means to circumvent the rules and find ever more exclusive and privileged ways of enacting their reproductive selves. I end with vignettes of some of the fascinating reproductive subjects emerging in today's rapidly changing environment.

One twenty-first-century figure is the self-directed, entrepreneurial "net-mom" who is actively constructing her identity as a modern, scientifically minded parent who mobilizes the technological resources of a globalizing economy to enhance her child-rearing skills.[45] On new parenting Web sites that are springing up, young mothers are self-consciously experimenting with new ways of being moms by exchanging experiences, creating home-pages for their babies, making friends, and even organizing offline activities with other netizens. Prioritizing their identity as parents over other identities, such as career women, they choose as their user names "so-and-so's mother" rather than their own name. They celebrate their generation's mothering as modern, independent thinking, global minded, and "happy," in contrast to the sacrificial motherhood of their own moms.

A second new figure is the Olympic baby. The Summer Olympics held in Beijing in August 2008 presented a unique opportunity for enterprising, self-managing parents desiring a child with global cachet. In November 2007, reproductive health centers around the country reported a huge boom in couples demanding *fuwa* babies—"babies of fortune"—who would be born between the Olympic dates of August 8 and 24 of the following year.[46] On the opening day of the Olympics, the Beijing Obstetrics and Gynecology Hospital experienced a 20 percent surge in deliveries.[47] Chinese numerology made that date especially auspicious: eight, *ba*, sounds like *fa*, the character for wealth. Babies born on 8/8/08 were babies of Olympic glory and triple fortune.

A third, currently salient, even fashionable, figure is the celebrity parent—of two or more children. Recently, as a booming economy has created a class of fabulously wealthy citizens, having several children has become a serious status symbol. Even as the poor must comply with the contraceptive and reproductive norms of the state to avoid heavy fines, film and sports stars are openly violating the one-child rule, happily paying the fines. Even the wealthy with no media cachet are using reproduction as an arena for the expression of class status. The 2001 Population and Birth Planning Law inadvertently facilitated this practice by dropping the earlier fine for noncompliance and substituting the Social Compensation Fee. This fee is understood as the compensation that excessively reproductive couples must pay to society for imposing on it the costly burden of an extra child. The wealthy openly violate the policy and have the child—simply because they can afford to. For them, the fee is merely an additional price that must be paid to achieve their desired family size.[48] The state, of course, is keen to stop these overt acts of defiance against the one-child-per-couple policy. In 2007 the Beijing government introduced steep new fines to discourage "excess" childbearing by celebrities. The football star Hao Haidong was fined 50,000 *yuan*—about $6,850—for having a second child. Municipal authorities explained that their concern was not so much demographic—after all, fertility is extremely low in China's cities—as cultural: they feared that, because of their fame, these stars' behavior would have "negative social influence."[49]

A final contemporary figure is the rich, pampered mom. In the 1980s and 1990s the "good mother" was the one who sacrificed herself and her family's economic well-being to give birth to a perfect child. The standard of care was the somber, if efficient and scientifically minded, state-run obstetric hospital.[50] As personal incomes have risen, the need to sacrifice the self has given way to a desire to pamper the self. The 2000s have seen the emergence of new spas catering to young mothers. In late 2007 a new 100-room center in Shanghai's Pudong District, which was converted from a luxury hotel, began providing tailored services—nursing, child care, dietary, beauty—from pre-birth to post-delivery. Despite the high cost—such services run 26,400 to 35,400 *yuan* ($3,600–$4,800) a month—demand is strong; expectant mothers of means are moving to Shanghai from neighboring provinces to avail themselves of the luxury services.[51]

The rise of a vital politics infused with a money ethic has led to the emergence of vast inequalities between the reproductive haves and have nots. Today the politics of reproduction is marked by growing gaps between city and village, coastal and interior regions, migrant and nonmigrant populations, and Han and non-Han groups, in everything from the quality of reproductive health care women receive to the number of children couples have, and the practices of child cultivation parents deploy. This trend is inverting the earlier class hierarchy of reproduction. Not long ago, it was the rural poor who had more children, and they did so because children, especially sons, were vital sources of labor and old-age support. Now, it seems to be the urban rich who are having more children, and children are becoming expensive consumer items and status symbols. Poor and rich also have different relationships to state policy. For the poor, the social compensation fee acts as a severe punishment, while for the wealthy it is a trivial expense. A globalizing China is also an increasingly unequal China in which even state policy sometimes privileges the rich.

An Increasingly Global Society—With Chinese Problems

The creators of China's population project sought to produce not only modern individuals, but also a modern society with the profile of a global power. Using the Western industrialized countries as their model, they aimed to eliminate demographic anomalies in the Chinese social body—in particular, the bumps in the age structure due to the post–Great Leap and Cultural Revolution baby booms—and create a society normalized to the Western standard. While succeeding in important ways, that massive project of individual and societal modernization has also created monumental problems that pose challenges both to individuals and families left behind in the race to modernity and to a state determined to optimize the development of China's society for nationalist ends.

An Increasingly Modern Society

Tables 2 and 3 compare China to major world regions and to individual global powers that China measures itself against. Table 2 details some results of the quantity project. By 2007 China's ultra-low fertility rate (1.73 children per woman, according to UN estimates) was very close to the average for the world's most developed regions (1.58). China's fertility rate was far below India's (2.79), and a little higher than Japan's and Russia's (both about 1.4). China's population growth rate was well above the average for the advanced countries, but only half that of the less-developed regions. Although the proportion of the population living in urban areas was well

Table 2 Population Quantity: China and Its Benchmark Countries

	Population (2007) (millions)	Population Growth Rate (2005–10)	Total Fertility Rate (2007)	Percent Population Urban	Urban Growth Rate (2005–10)
China	1,331.4	.6	1.73 (UN figure)	42	2.7
India	1,135.6	1.4	2.79	29	2.3
Japan	128.3	.1	1.36	66	.4
Russia	141.9	−.4	1.40	73	−.6
United States	303.9	.9	2.04	81	1.3
World	6,615.9	1.1	2.56	50	2.0
More Dvd Regions	1,217.5	.2	1.58	75	.5
Less Dvd	5,398.4	1.3	2.76	44	2.5
Least Dvd Regions	795.6	2.3	4.74	28	4.0

Source: United Nations Population Fund, *State of World Population 2007*, at www.unfpa.org, Table on Demographic, Social, and Economic Indicators.

below the rates for the United States, Russia, and Japan (42 percent compared to 81, 73, and 66 percent, respectively), it was considerably higher than India's (29 percent). With an urban growth rate of 2.7 percent, China can be expected to catch up in good time. In many ways, the PRC has gone a remarkable way toward achieving a "global, modern" society. On all these measures, China has maintained its strong lead over India, long a symbol of the kind of third-world backwardness China wants to escape.

Table 3 displays some results of the quality project on population. The PRC's efforts to produce a competitive labor force and a modern citizenry have paid off in rising levels of child and, in turn, population health and education. China's infant and child mortality rates, while remaining high relative to the levels of the high-income industrialized countries, are now about half the levels of the middle-income regions and of India. The proportion of young children who are underweight for their age is a remarkably low 8 percent; the comparable figure for India is 47 percent (numbers not shown). Life expectancy at birth, a good measure of overall health, is an extraordinary 72.5 years (for males and females together), a figure falling

Table 3 Population "Quality:" China and Its Benchmark Countries

A. Health

	GDP per capita (2005) (PPP US$)	Life Expect. at Birth (2005)	Life Expect. at Birth, f/m	Infant Mortality (under 1) per 1,000 live births	Infant+Child Mortality (under 5) per 1,000 live births, m/f
China	6,757	72.5	74.3/71.0	31	30/41
India	3,452	63.7	65.3/62.3	60	84/88
Japan	31,267	82.3	85.7/78.7	3	5/4
Russia	10,845	65.0	72.1/58.6	16	24/18
United States	41,890	77.9	80.4/75.2	7	8/8
World	9,543	68.1	—	53	80/77
High-Income Regions	33,082	79.2	—	7*	10/9*
Middle- Income Regions	7,416	70.9	—	58*	87/85*
Low-Income Regions	2,531	60.0	—	92*	155/144*

Notes: Except where otherwise listed, all data are for 2007. Gross Domestic Product per capita is in Parity Purchasing Power US$.

* Data for more developed, less developed, and least developed regions

Sources: GDP and life expectancy data from United Nations Development Program, *Human Development Report 2007–2008*, at http://hdr.undp.org, Tables 1 and 28. Infant and child mortality data from United Nations Population Fund, *State of World Population 2007*, at www.unfpa.org, Tables on Demographic, Social, and Economic Indicators and Monitoring ICPD Goals.

B. Education

	Adult Literacy	Combined Gross Enrollment, Primary, Secondary, and Tertiary Levels	Combined Enrollment, female/male
China	90.9	69.1	69/70
India	61.0	63.8	60/68
Japan	–	85.9	85/87
Russia	99.4	88.9	93/85
United States	–	93.3	98/89
World	78.6	67.8	–
High-Income Regions	–	92.3	–
Middle-Income Regions	89.9	73.3	–
Low-Income Regions	60.2	56.3	–

Notes: Adult literacy is percentage of population aged 15 and above who are literate, 1995–2005.

Sources: United Nations Development Program, *Human Development Report 2007–2008*, at http://hdr.undp.org, Tables 1 and 28.

midway between the life expectancy of the global leaders Japan and the U.S. (82.3 and 77.9, respectively), and the global laggards Russia and India (65.0 and 63.7, respectively). Despite persistent gaps in the survival of young girls and boys, child survival prospects overall have continued to improve in the reform decades.[52]

Advances in education, crucial to the development of a knowledge-based economy, are equally noteworthy. The proportion of primary, secondary, and tertiary school-age Chinese children that are enrolled in school is 69.1 percent, with small differences between boys and girls. Adult literacy has reached a remarkable 90.9 percent, with 86.5 percent of women and 95.1 percent of men able to read. This compares very favorably with the global adult literacy level of 78.6 percent and the Indian rate of 61 percent. Although the educational advances have been unequally distributed, with the urban population benefitting much more than the rural people and the coastal areas more than the hinterland regions of western and central China, overall they have been impressive. Working with other policy efforts, the birth policy has helped produce that young, capable workforce that has made China such a competitive actor in the global economy.

Big challenges remain, however, especially given the worldwide shift toward knowledge as the basis for national competitiveness that has followed the so-called global knowledge and information revolution. If the regime's World Bank advisors are right, China will be able to remain competitive only if it responds to these changes by further increasing enrollment in secondary and tertiary education, modernizing its curriculum, and reducing regional inequalities in educational opportunities.[53]

Table 4 compares the achievements of China and its major strategic competitors on an aggregate measure of human development, the UN's human development index. This measure represents the average of three indices—on life expectancy, education, and standard of living (measured as GDP per capita).[54] Although an index such as this represents a limited measure of real human development (defined by the United Nations as a widening of the options available to people), it is a useful general indicator nonetheless. In 2005, the highest human development score was 97 (of 100; that score belonged to Iceland), the lowest 34 (Sierra Leone). In 1980, China's human development index was a mere 56, higher than India's 45 but still far below Japan's and America's 89. By 2005, the PRC had increased its lead over India,

Table 4   Human Development Index: China and Its Benchmark Countries (100 is
maximum)

	1980	2005	Change, 1980–2005
China	55.9	77.7	+21.8
India	45.0	61.9	+16.9
Japan	88.6	95.3	+6.7
Russia	—	80.2	—
United States	89.0	95.1	+6.1

Source: United Nations Development Program, *Human Development Report 2007–2008*,
at http://hdr.undp.org, Table 1.

almost caught up with Russia, and begun to close the gap between itself and
the leading powers, Japan and the United States. In those twenty-five years,
China boosted its HDI by 21.8 points. India raised its human index by 16.9
points, while Japan and the United States increased theirs by 6 to 7 points.
Measured in such aggregated numbers, China's grand national project on
human development would seem to be paying off.

"Backward" Persons

The process of reproductive normalization has created not only individuals
who fit the scientific standards, but also deviants, persons unable or perhaps
unwilling to live by the societal norms. Despite the growing importance of
market forces in shaping reproductive subjects in China, the official norms
guiding what constitutes socially valued forms of sex, marriage, and reproduction have remained remarkably durable. As we have seen, these norms
have been quite restrictive. Whole categories of people who in other contexts might have lived good, if nonconformist, lives have been excluded
from the state's regime of social welfare and social virtue. Given the moral
judgments associated with conformity to the dominant norms, members of
groups outside the norms have tended to live difficult and often stigmatized
lives. Where the state has imposed economic, political, and/or legal sanctions on unapproved categories—a step it has rarely hesitated to take—the
human and material costs of "deviance" have been even greater. Of course,
many have tried to challenge their relegation to the social margins. Stories

of individual struggles suggest that the road to social approbation and support is usually long.

This is not the place for an exhaustive list of all the categories of persons that have been excluded from the state's post-1978 regime of reproductive modernity. Indeed, making such a list would be impossible: not only are new categories of modern/backward citizens frequently being created, but the old categories are constantly being redefined or reworked in response to changed conditions. Moreover, the number of "backward" groups is potentially very large. Instead, I simply describe a handful of the major categories of "backwardness." In doing so, I hope to convey a sense of the nature and scope of the problems of social deviance, and of the forms of exclusion to which those so labeled are subject.

Perhaps the major categories of "nonmodern" individuals are those who represent "too high quantity" or "too low quality" in the state's scheme of social virtue. One huge category of "deviants" includes couples who violated the policy on number of births and carried an unauthorized pregnancy to term. According to state statistics—which certainly understate the extent of the problem—in the 1980s fully 32 percent of all births were "unplanned" or illegitimate; by the late 1990s that number had fallen to 7 percent.[55] As we have seen, couples who have defied the birth rules have been subject to strong state sanctions. Their unplanned offspring—widely known as "black children" *(hei haizi)*—have suffered even more. Even as planned single children have been showered with state support, unplanned children lacking household registration have been treated as nonpersons and deprived of all state benefits, from the right to schooling and basic health care to the legal right to work, marry, and even die.[56]

Another massive category includes persons deemed "low in quality." Whole classes of people—rural residents, rural migrants to the cities, women, minorities, and those with substandard bodies, for example—have been labeled low in quality and obstacles to the nation's modernization effort. Some "low-quality" citizens (such as women) have been targeted for energetic, state-sponsored improvement campaigns, while others (rural people, for example) have been essentially abandoned as useless to the modernization effort.[57]

A third type of "unmodern" person includes those who reject the conventional norms on reproduction, sexuality, and marriage. Gays, gay couples and parents, unmarried adults, childless adults, and so forth tend to live lives of social exclusion and face intense social pressure to conform.[58] One category that has received considerable media attention in the 2000s is the unmarried mother. Teenage girls, who have been actively experimenting with sex, are some of the major users of the state's abortion services, because being an unmarried mother, especially a teenage mother, is socially unthinkable, even in China's cities. Women in their twenties and thirties who wish to have a child out of wedlock encounter not only social stigmatization, but also legal barriers: in most of the country, it is illegal to conceive a child outside of marriage. Women who manage to give birth are treated as social outcasts and encounter endless problems trying to raise the child on their own. The exception seems to be women with economic means in very liberal cities such as Shanghai, which guarantees the rights of children born outside marriage. Although the issue of single motherhood has been slow to enter the public arena, there is growing awareness of the plight of such women and the need for legal and cultural reform.[59]

An Unequal Society

The project of rapid modernization has also produced wrenching effects at the level of society as a whole. Since the 1980s, the state's overzealous attempts to avert a demographic crisis have produced (or worsened) two social crises that are arguably at least as severe as the original crisis of high fertility: a severely distorted sex ratio among the young and a rapidly aging society largely lacking social security. These two trends carry ominous implications for China's future. At 120 boys per 100 girls (in 2007), China's highly imbalanced sex ratio at birth far outstrips the international average of 105 to 106.[60] This national average, worrying though it is, understates the extent of the problem in some areas. In 1999–2000, the sex ratio at birth exceeded 130 in Anhui, Hubei, Guangdong, and Hainan provinces. A more fine-grained, county-level analysis of the sex ratio among children aged 0 to 4 reveals a national average of 120.2, but spatial clusters of counties in which the ratio ranges from 150 to 197.2:100. In those areas, scattered around east, central, and south China, there are now three or four boys for every two girls. In 2000, a worrying 40 percent of China's people lived in counties with a seriously imbalanced sex ratio of 120 or above, while 5 percent resided in counties with ratios above 150.[61]

How will this growing gender gap play out socially as these new, male-heavy generations of youngsters grow older? It is too early to say, but the evidence to date suggests that the changes are likely to be wrenching. According to one estimate, 23 million young men already born will not be able to marry in the culturally preferred way.[62] Chinese sources routinely warn that by 2020, some 30 million Chinese men will be unable to find brides. In 2008, Population Minister Li Bin warned that if the sex ratio at birth remains at the current level through 2020, one in five Chinese men will be unable to marry.[63] But they are finding ways to do so. Especially in poorer areas, the dearth of brides has led to the large-scale kidnapping and purchase of women, the importation of brides from poorer countries, and the emergence of culturally despised forms of union, including polyandrous marriages in which one woman services two or more men. Those who are unable to find brides in these or other ways may have no marriage prospects at all. These men may live together in bachelor communities or form a spatially dispersed bachelor underclass.

Since the early 2000s, the growing gender gap has become a very serious policy concern among China's leaders. Conversations in Beijing suggest that throughout the population establishment, both officials and their scholarly advisors remain deeply concerned about this issue as well. The 2007 Decision calls for comprehensive efforts to address both current problems and their root causes. Beyond legally forbidding prenatal sex determination and sex-selective abortion for nonmedical reasons—rules that have been on the books since the early 1990s but still lack effective enforcement measures—the birth establishment has initiated a wide range of activities designed to eliminate discrimination against girls and women and improve their status in the family and society. These include a massive propaganda effort—"Introducing New Concepts on Marriage and Childbearing to Millions of Households"—aimed at reducing son preference and promoting gender equality; wide-ranging programs to improve job and other opportunities for women; and a much-publicized Action to Foster (or Care for) Girls designed to boost their well-being through preferential treatment (in poverty reduction, charity assistance, subsidized loans, and employment, for example) for rural girl-child families that have accepted birth planning. On the legal front, the state has stepped up efforts to strengthen laws against the abandonment of infant girls and the discrimination against, kidnapping, and trafficking of women. It has worked hard to popularize legal knowledge about the protection of the legitimate rights and interests of women and children.[64] Yet with few truly effective solutions in sight, and a larger culture and political economy that in many ways support discrimination against girls and women, restoring the sex ratio to normal seems a very long-term prospect. Indeed, undoing the sexism embedded in China's culture and political economy may well lie beyond the power of the state.

China also faces a near-term future of rapid aging because of the speed of fertility decline and the continued rise in life expectancy. In 2005 a relatively low 7.6 percent of China's people were 65 and older, but the aging of China's population will accelerate. According to UN projections, that figure can be expected to triple or quadruple to 20, 24, or 28 percent by 2050, depending on future fertility.[65] By comparison, today the proportion of the population aged 65 and over is 12 percent in the United States, 16 percent in the United Kingdom, 19 percent in Germany, and 20 percent in Japan. In aging, as in all demographic dynamics in China, there is a sharp urban–rural gradient. Because of the earlier urban implementation of the one-child policy, the cities are growing old much faster than the villages.

The growing number of Chinese elderly is cause for concern because two essential support systems—the public pension and health care insurance systems—are ill prepared for the increase. In the early 2000s, only 25 percent of the workforce had any kind of pension. (In the cities the figure was 55 percent, but in the villages only 11 percent.) Today fully 40 percent of urban residents and 80 percent of rural villagers have no health care coverage at all. With the costs of medical care rising rapidly, health care for the elderly often imposes a huge burden on family resources.[66] The government's overall approach to the aging problem, outlined in the 2007 Decision, calls for proactively responding by establishing an old-age social security system that is based on family care for the aged, supported by community services, and supplemented by institutional services for seniors.[67] In the urban areas, where the decline in the state-owned sector is creating huge gaps in the network of public support for retired workers, the emphasis is on developing markets of products and services for the aged. The population and birth commission has already taken some big steps in rural social security work.

In 2004 it introduced an important new initiative that provides rural couples aged 60 and over who had sacrificed for birth planning by having only one child or two daughters with a modest monthly pension. This system was extended countrywide in 2007.[68] This initiative is useful, but it addresses only a portion of the old-age-support problem. Lacking public pensions, most of China's seniors must depend on their families to protect them from impoverishment and support them in times of declining health. Yet as birth rates continue to decline and youth migrate elsewhere for better jobs, the family support network for the aged is being strained to the limit. Specialists on aging worry that unless China is able to put together an effective nationwide retirement system very soon, starting around 2015 the country will experience an old-age support crisis so severe it might threaten China's plans to become a world power.[69]

3

Strengthening China's Party-State and Place in the World

The governance of population through modern science and technology has been central to the rise of global China. In the last chapter, I described the creation of global persons and a global society. I turn now to the effects of the rise of vital politics on the party-state and on China's position in the world. Population governance both challenges and complicates standard views of the party-state under reform.

Conventional wisdom in China political science is that the marketizing reforms inaugurated in the late 1970s have led to a decline in the scope and intensity of state power. In hopes of enhancing its effectiveness and legitimacy, the party-state has withdrawn from its intrusive penetration of society, relaxing its control over growing portions of the social, economic, political, and intellectual life of the citizenry. At the same time, some of the party's traditional Leninist instruments of control (propaganda, coercion, and organization, for example) have eroded. The result has been a general decrease in state power over society.[1] These widely shared conclusions have given rise to a lively debate on the implications for the PRC regime. For some, the party and governing apparatus appear endangered, and the party-state itself at risk of disintegration.[2] With the rise of a more confident China in recent years, however, growing numbers of analysts are seeing not state retreat or retrenchment, but rather successful adaptation to a complex domestic and international environment. In this view, the party-state is becoming both more flexible and more capable and competent in its ability to govern. Looking at China today, these observers see a remarkably resilient regime of authoritarian government. If China can find effective solutions to the serious challenges it now faces—institutional deficiencies; fragile social stability; a still-large and backward population; vast income, health, and educational inequalities; and low political participation, for example—that regime of authoritarian government should be sustainable over the next few decades.[3]

What happens to these arguments when we expand the field of politics to include population, and use more anthropological notions of power and politics that take not only institutions, but also discourse, subjectivity, science, and the body as central objects of critical inquiry? Those are the questions I address here. Population supports the arguments of successful adaptation to an increasingly complex environment and growing capacity to govern effectively.[4] Through our study of changing modes of subjectification, in Chapter 2 we saw a ragged but very real process of learning from the mistakes of the coercive 1980s and a shift to less costly, more market-based techniques of administering the population and creating the modern workers and citizens that are crucial to the party's larger agenda.

Yet population lends little support to the idea that state power in social and economic domains has atrophied. Quite the contrary. Given its centrality to the modernizing projects of the post-Mao regime, from the beginning population has been a field in which the state has insisted on retaining power and on micromanaging the demographic transition and the creation of a quality populace. Work on modern power suggests that the effects of projects of population optimization will be mostly unpredicted, and in China they truly were. In ways that the reform state surely did not intend, population has been a highly productive site for the buildup of state power, the securing of regime legitimacy, and the creation of new, more subtle forms of power exercised at the level of the biological body. Population governance has also influenced China's global position in ways the regime certainly did not plan. The population project has complicated China's efforts to be seen as a responsible stakeholder in the global system. At the same time, the regime's success in upgrading the populace has facilitated China's rise to global prominence and power. Achievements in the population arena have made a substantial contribution to China's ability to boost its Comprehensive National Power (CNP)—the favored measure of national might—and close the gap between China and today's sole superpower, the United

States. I begin this story in the late 1970s, when this new project on life was taking root.

A Stronger, More Capable Party-State

For post-Mao leaders, population presented an optimal domain in which to strengthen a socialist state that had been greatly weakened by the disasters of the late-Mao era. The reasons, described elsewhere, were several.[5] Although population growth rates had fallen markedly during the last few years of Mao's rule, the chairman's reformist successors deemed his "failure to control population growth" one of his most grievous mistakes. By taking firm control over this domain, Deng-era leaders could both "rectify an historical error" committed by the party and demonstrate the ability of their modernizing regime to solve one of the most basic problems in China's development—and transform China's backward masses into a modern populace at last. Population was also an appealing arena because, unlike other domains of governance—"culture," "society," or "the economy," for example— "population" was defined as a biological object requiring a governmental approach based on modern science. The centrality of modern science to managing the population problem allowed the state to foster the development of a cluster of new population-related sciences, and to present itself as a scientific modernizer committed to using modern S&T to ameliorate China's problems. Population was also an appealing domain for rebuilding the state because population processes unfolded over extended periods of time and were closely tied to social and economic development. Sound population planning and policymaking thus required the sorts of comprehensive, short- and long-term planning capabilities that were the hallmark of the socialist state. The sheer statistical complexity of managing China's gargantuan population required the buildup of a large data-gathering and processing capacity centered in the state and affiliated institutions. In 1979–1980, the creators of the new population project began to construct an enormous edifice of knowledge and state power that sought to take charge of the production and, to a lesser extent, cultivation of life itself. In this section I examine three dimensions of this state-building process: institutional, legal, and governmental.

Population and State Strengthening: Institutional Dimensions

Since the rise of Deng Xiaoping, population has been the site for an extraordinary buildup of power centered in the party-state. Key to that process was the ostensibly scientific construction of the population problem as a "crisis of modernization" that not only kept China backward, a framing we have encountered before, but also threatened the well-being of the world at large. Resolving this "national and international crisis" rooted in biological excess—too many Chinese—required a strong regime with the political will and might, the scientific knowledge, and the globalist vision and sense of responsibility necessary to "save" the nation from backwardness—and the world from overpopulation—through the firm control of population growth. Frequently referencing this urgent rationale, and updating it with new and frightening numbers, China's population planners set out to create precisely that kind of state.

As a result of these efforts, over the last three decades population has become the site for an extraordinary expansion of state power in the social domain. As we saw in Chapter 1, the realm of population/social policy has grown ever larger, and now includes gender, aging, social security, and health, as well as population quantity and quality, to say nothing of migration, which I have not addressed here. Resolving these problems has been politically productive, involving the construction of a sprawling, multilevel network of governmental agencies and related organizations. The centerpiece has been the State Birth Planning Commission, established in 1981 to manage the newly uncovered crisis at the heart of China's modernization project. Set up to coordinate key party and government agencies involved in population work, the State Birth Planning Commission lay at the apex of a hierarchy of birth planning commissions and committees extending all the way down the administrative structure. A parallel structure of party committees held ultimate decision-making power at each level. In 2003, just as population policy was being transformed into broad social policy, the Commission was enlarged and renamed the National Population and Birth Planning Commission.

In the intervening years, those in charge of population have created a huge network of affiliated governmental and (nominally) nongovernmental organizations to facilitate the optimal management of China's population.

Table 5   A Buildup of Organizations to Manage the Population

National Population and Family Planning Commission of China
Major affiliated organizations:
  National Family Planning Research Institute
  China Population and Development Research Center
  National Center for Contraceptives Development
  China Population News
  China Population Publishing House
  Logistic Service Center
  China Population Communication Center
  Training and Communication Center
  Nanjing International Population Training Center

Major NGOs:
  China Family Planning Association
  China Population Welfare Association
  China Population Association
  China Population Culture Promotion Association

Note: "Family planning" is the official translation for *jihua shengyu,* which is more correctly rendered as "birth planning."
Source: NPFPC Web site, www.nfppc.gov.cn.

The major organizations in charge of administering China's population can be found in Table 5. This list does not include the large number of research centers devoted to gathering and analyzing demographic data. Centers of demographic research exist in government bureaucracies (the National Bureau of Statistics, the State Development and Planning Commission, and the Public Security Bureau, among others), universities, social science academies, and party schools.

According to official records, at the beginning of 2006, China had no fewer than 82,340 organizations devoted to population and family planning work. Of these, 13 were national organizations, 252 provincial, 1,799 prefectural, 10,730 county, and 69,556 township-level entities.[6] These organizations were staffed by three-quarters of a million workers. These numbers included 508,713 "personnel" (or staff), 104,753 "public servants" (presumably state and party cadres), and 161,541 "professionals." Of the experts, 135,109 were health workers. Many of the other professionals apparently were researchers. With the government's emphasis on improving the educational qualifications of public-sector workers, the educational level of

population and family planning personnel has increased dramatically in
recent years. Official data on these personnel show that in early 2006, 74.7
percent of public servants and 46.5 percent of professionals had college
or higher levels of education. Five years earlier, in 2001, only 53.4 percent
of public servants and 39.1 percent of professionals had college degrees.
Population/family planning work seems to be a predominantly female pro-
fession, though men hold the majority of managerial roles. At the beginning of 2006, 56.7 percent of personnel (staff), 40.9 percent of public servants, and 76.7 percent of professionals (i.e., medical workers) were women.

A Growing Terrain of Socialist Legality

Solving the population problem has also entailed the formation of a new
and ever-growing terrain of socialist legality. In the 1970s, birth work operated on the basis of informal party and state mechanisms; there were no
formal, central-level policies that had the imprimatur of top party and government bodies. Since 1979 population governance has been guided by increasingly formal legal means. Initially, population law was embodied in
other legal instruments, such as the 1978 and 1982 Constitutions of the PRC
and the 1982 Marriage Law. As population work became more complex,
national laws were developed to handle specific population-related problems. For example, the Criminal Law of 1979 (revised in 1997) dealt with the
theft of babies and the abduction and trafficking of women; the Law on Protection of Minors (1991) dealt with the protection of the physical and mental
health of children; the Adoption Law (1991, revised in 1998) handled the
adoption of children; the Law on Protecting the Legal Rights and Interests
of Women (1992, revised in 2005) dealt with a range of women's issues; the
Maternal and Infant Health Care Law (1994, originally called the Eugenics
Law, a name that was roundly criticized) covered eugenic (that is, genetic
and biological) issues; and the Law on the Protection of the Rights and Interests of the Elderly (1996) outlined legal approaches to ensuring the welfare of China's growing aged population. In 2001, after more than twenty
years of contentious debate, the Standing Committee of the National People's
Congress finally passed the nation's first national law on population and
birth planning.[7] Since the Tenth Five-Year Plan period (2001–2005), legal
development has continued, producing such documents as the Methods on

Population and Birth Planning Work among the Floating Population; the Regulations on Birth Planning Technical and Service Management; and the Methods on Collection of Social Compensation Fee.[8] A review of laws enacted in other sectors would reveal many more items dealing with core population issues. Today, nearly ten years after the promulgation of the historic birth planning law, "administration by law" is considered the basic demand for good work in the population and birth planning programs.[9]

Of course, the addition of a new arena of governance almost invariably results in the creation of new institutions and laws. Yet population was an extreme case. Because the dynamics of population growth were so poorly understood and because the core policy on population was so flawed, efforts to enforce that policy produced problem after problem, forcing officials in the state to be constantly struggling to create new rules, regulations, and eventually laws to deal with them. The result was an especially rapid buildup of institutional and legal power in the state. Of course, the mere promulgation of these laws does not mean they have been effectively enforced; quite the contrary, poor or spotty enforcement has been a major stumbling block to China's post-Mao legal development generally. Yet the creation of legal instruments is an important first step, signaling state concern about an ever-widening set of population-related problems and providing a relatively firm basis on which enforcement efforts can build.

In the Chinese setup, the political Center issues general guidelines on births and on population work, leaving the formulation of concrete rules and regulations to the provinces. China's roughly thirty provinces, municipalities, and autonomous regions have issued several rounds of birth planning regulations, beginning in the late 1970s. Each time the Center modifies the birth policy, the provinces must revise and reissue their regulations. In addition to these core national and provincial instruments, those seeking to govern China's population have found it useful and/or necessary to create a wide range of other documents. As the problem of population has grown more complex and the difficulties of enforcement have multiplied, there has emerged an ever-widening array of documents dedicated to specific political and governmental ends. This is not the place for a detailed analysis of these materials, but a simple list of the types of documents issued can suggest the legal complexity of this domain. At the central level, these have ranged from white papers rationalizing the official approach, to ten-year

strategies to map out past achievements and future goals; technical enforcement rules to guide implementation; and more informal opinions,
decisions, notifications, and circulars often designed to circumvent the
long, cumbersome process of making legislative changes. At the provincial
and subprovincial levels there has been a welter of such documents, aimed
at clarifying the existing birth rules, adding new specifications to existing
rules, making short-term rule changes, addressing thorny issues, articulat-
ing the rules for the collection and use of penalty payments, modifying the
reward and penalty system, establishing procedures for special groups, or
settling administrative questions such as the procedures for printing, sign-
ing, sealing, checking, and filing of documents. Some idea of the documentary productivity of the birth program can be gleaned from the results of a
mid-1990s campaign to rectify local birth norms: in the seventeen provinces in which the campaign began, more than 50,000 documents were
located.[10]

A Growing Capacity to Govern

Since the mid-1990s, population has been a site not only for state strengthening, but also for state learning, that is, for the incubation and trial adoption of new and sometimes highly effective techniques of governance. In
the 1980s and early 1990s, of course, population management was a prime
example of bad governance, even by the regime's own standards, which
have consistently rejected the use of what in party-speak is called "coercion and commandism." Although the state has always given top priority
to the demographic ends of lowering population growth and stabilizing
population size, as the demography has improved, China's population
governors have been able to pay more attention to the means by which
they govern.

    Some students of Chinese politics have argued that over the reform years,
even as the state has narrowed its governing focus, it has come to govern the
areas of persistent interest more effectively and efficiently.[11] A study of population governance, especially since the early 1990s, supports this conclusion and suggests that population has been at the forefront of that trend.
Because of the scope and difficulty of the task, and because the stakes have
been deemed so high, the regime has devoted extraordinary effort, year

after year, to getting the governance of population right. Over the years the field of population governance has effectively served as a seedbed for the invention of new ideas and techniques of human governance in a rapidly globalizing society. Although I have been able to mention only a few of the techniques by which the state has sought to define and manage the population problem, the discussion of methods of creating reproductive subjects in the last chapter suggests the creative, trial-and-error nature of the process. Enormous attention has also been devoted to techniques for managing government population and birth cadres.

In the years since 1980, the state has at first fitfully, and later more dependably abandoned Maoist techniques that have been costly or counterproductive, while adapting to a rapidly changing environment by embracing new neoliberal-type modes of governance that incorporate market techniques and shift responsibilities from the state to local communities and individuals. These methods of governance are potentially more effective and efficient because they transfer responsibilities from the state to increasingly self-directed, self-governing communities and individuals, saving state resources; because they draw on knowledge of social and cultural dynamics to tap people's own resourcefulness and powers of self-making; because they intervene at the level of desire, trying to align individual desires with state agendas; and because they substitute service-oriented for administrative approaches, reducing popular hostility to state projects. Perhaps ironically, as population numbers have shrunk, state capacity to manage them well appears to have grown.

Governing Through Biology: A New, Embodied Form of Power

The conventional wisdom on state power in China—that its scope and intensity are shrinking—neglects the power dynamics involved in governing the population. To be sure, students of Chinese politics have long considered population an exception, a "hard" policy arena in which state controls remain strong, even as they have loosened in other domains of social and economic life. Here I mean something different. Based on a biological view of the social world, China's population project defines and governs men and women through their reproductive biologies. In operating this way, the governance of population has produced a qualitatively new form of power that is exercised at the level of the individual biological body and collective species body. This form of power—known, following Foucault, as bio-power—is the calculated power over life, especially at the level of the population. It is aimed at the administration of the vital characteristics of human populations and exercised not for the repressive end of enhancing control, but for the more positive end of optimizing the population's health, welfare, and life. Foucault maintained that biopower is the characteristic form that power assumes in the modern era, when biological life itself becomes a central object of power. Biopower has particular implications for women's bodies and lives, though Foucault was not interested in that feature.

The rise of Chinese biopower has involved the increased management and ordering of biological life itself. In the governance of population quantity, the aggregate population has been turned into an object of study, intervention, and control aimed at manipulating its fertility, mortality, morbidity, and other vital rates so as to eliminate deviations in the species body. Irregularities in the age and sex structure, the dispersion of bodies across space, the rates of fertility and net increase, and other biological features are all subject to management so as to produce an optimal social body modeled on the scientific norm. At the individual level, governing through biology has entailed taking charge of the female reproductive body, making it the object of knowledge, surveillance, regulation, and control. By defining womanhood essentially in terms of motherhood, and motherhood in terms of reproductive physiology, these efforts have reshaped the bodies, lives, and identities of virtually all Chinese women of childbearing age. In their efforts to improve population quality, the state and growing numbers of social agents have transformed the body of the child, before and after birth, into an object of the same types of governmental processes, all aimed at optimizing its genetic and biological makeup.

These bodily interventions have also extended the scope of state power.[12] In the literature on China's birth control program, the 825 million IUD insertions, IUD removals, abortions, and sterilizations that by the early 2000s had been conducted on women's (and, to a much lesser extent, men's) bodies are treated as matters of contraceptive prevalence and reproductive health. The larger political significance of this surgical effort has gone unremarked. Yet each of these state-mandated surgeries is a serious political act that has extended the reach of the state to a place it had never gone in the Mao era, when the state sought to push its tentacles into every corner of Chinese life. State power now reaches not only into the bedroom, intruding on sexual negotiations and reproductive deliberations that had long belonged to the sphere of the patriarchal family. It also stretches into the womb, deemed the wellspring of generativity for the woman, her kin, and the community. With its intervention in population, the state has penetrated to the biological and symbolic core of Chinese society, taking unto itself fearsome new powers that go beyond the remaking of the family—the goal of the Maoist state—to the making of life itself.

The Discursive Power of "Population"

The expansion of state power around population can also be traced in the discursive domain. I discuss here the cultural and political power of just three aspects of population discourse: party slogans, program categories, and the official narrative of the party saving China from a demographic crisis.

Party Slogans and Cultural Change

As is typical for China, solving this state-defined problem has led to the invention of a colorful and ever-growing array of party slogans. Slogans about population have rarely been dropped; instead, as the policy and program have shifted, their meanings have been subtly reworked. Some slogans, which might be called program slogans, are directed at cadres throughout the birth planning apparatus. Important program slogans have included "the three basics" (early 1980s), "open a small hole to close a large hole" (1984), "the three unchangings" (early 1990s), "the two transformations" (mid-1990s), provide "quality service" (mid-1990s), and "taking people as the core" (late 1990s, early 2000s). As every practicing cadre knows, each of these program slogans (and a great many others) signals important emphases in population work or critical shifts in the party line on population, must-attend-to's that are ignored at one's peril.

Others are policy slogans directed at the people: "advocate one child per couple," "practice late marriage and delayed childbearing," "have one, quality child," and "girl or boy, both are the same" are common examples. Although party slogans such as these tend to be neglected by students of Chinese social life, slogan-making has social and political effects that matter. Delivering propaganda and education is a major function of the birth planning establishment, one that it has consistently addressed with utmost seriousness. Over the decades the birth commission has devoted inordinate attention to creating compelling slogans and making them a ubiquitous part of Chinese life. Because the state controls the means of public communication, its messages can have extraordinary effects. As visitors to China have frequently noted, since around 1980 slogans promoting the one-child policy have been widely propagandized—on billboards and building walls, in schools, in the mass media, in parenting books and magazines, and more. Slogans that are part of people's everyday environment month after month, year after year, gradually lose their status as political slogan and become part of popular culture. When doing fieldwork in rural Shaanxi in the late 1980s, I was astonished to see the birth planning slogan "have only one child" prominently displayed at a local wedding. Seeing it as an unwelcome intrusion of the state into people's private lives, I gingerly asked the bride about it. She smiled and said she had not even noticed it; it was "just the way things are done now." By defining the population problem as a crisis of too many Chinese requiring a patriotic response, and by associating tiny families with modernity, the state's propaganda and education efforts have been major forces for cultural change.

Not everyone accepts the state's messages on population at face value, of course. In the cities today, young, educated people are taking advantage of the anonymity of the Internet to satirize the state's earlier, harsh approach to population control. Bloggers are ridiculing slogans like "Raise fewer babies but more piglets" and "One baby means one more tomb," prompting the birth commission to undertake a major campaign to soften the program's image (described earlier).[13] Yet the state has already established the terms of discourse, the language and framing in which population issues are discussed and understood. Bloggers can poke fun at the official slogans and the state can soften its touch, but the larger, state-produced discourse on population—with its assumptions that reproduction is a matter of state, that the one-child policy is China's "only choice," and that all have a patriotic duty to limit their childbearing—remains intact.

Categorizing Chinese Life, Creating Chinese Personhood

The development of population governance has also entailed the proliferation of categories of enforcement. Historically, the central categories focused on the timing and number of children. Familiar classifications included authorized and unauthorized pregnancies; early and late marriage and childbearing; first, second, and "multiple" births; and so on. Every modification in policy and program direction has brought new categories to the fore. Because population work is now guided by law, these categories tend to have legal or quasi-legal force. The 2001 national population law, for example, includes categories of safe/unsafe birth control operations (Article 19); women who do/do not give birth to female infants; fertile/infertile women; female infants who are/are not mistreated or abandoned (Article 22); citizens who do/do not undergo birth control surgery (Article 26); parents whose only child does/does not suffer accidental disability or death and who do/do not later give birth to or adopt another child (Article 27); couples who voluntarily decide to have only one child (Article 27); households that are/are not poverty-stricken (Article 28), and those who do/do not use ultrasound to detect the sex of their fetus and terminate the pregnancy for other than medical reasons (Article 36).[14] The 2007 Decision pays particular attention to rural girl-child families: couples whose only child is injured, disabled, or has died; infants with birth defects; and women who resort to sex-selective abortion.[15] These categories apply to "clients" of the birth program; there is a parallel universe of categories for birth and population workers.

The human import of this multiplication of categories must not be lost. As life has been divided up into more, and more minutely ranked, classifications, growing numbers of people and behaviors have become objects of state monitoring, data gathering, administrative management, and political control. Attached to each of these categories is a set of rewards (or penalties) that encourage people to comply with prescribed behaviors. Typical benefits include post-surgical and maternity leave; living allowances; old-age support, social support, and social insurance schemes such as basic pension insurance, basic medical insurance, childbirth insurance, and social welfare; and priority in receiving housing allocations, poverty relief, job and technical training, charity assistance, and subsidized loans. There is a similar, though much shorter, list of penalties for noncompliance. Couples who

comply gain not only material benefits but also, potentially, social connections, political rewards, and other benefits. While some are certainly reluc-
tant acceptors of the reproductive rules, others are becoming active agents
of personal change. Just as, in the wake of the Chernobyl catastrophe, Ukrai-
nians affected by the disaster claimed rights to state benefits based on a new
"biological citizenship," in China some are taking advantage of the designa-
tions in the birth program to claim rights to new state resources.[16] Like the
general classes of reproductive subjectivity we examined earlier ("the good
mother," "the quality child"), these program categories have had deep effects not just on people's reproductive behavior, but on their identities and
social, economic, and political well-being as well.

A Permanent Crisis and an Enduring Support to Party Legitimacy

Population governance has also benefitted the party that continues to domi-
nate state and society alike. Perhaps most importantly, the population project has helped to undergird the legitimacy of the CCP.[17] Despite overseeing
the extraordinary growth of China's economy, in the early twenty-first century the ruling party's legitimacy remains "brittle," as one observer has put
it, threatened by widespread social protest, party-state corruption, gaping
inequality, and other problems.[18] In a rapidly changing domestic and international environment, securing its right to rule is an ever-present concern
for the CCP. Students of CCP politics have argued that the party today is
seeking to secure its legitimacy by positioning itself as the sole guarantor
of three things: continued economic growth, sociopolitical stability; and
nationalistic pride in China and its accomplishments.[19]

The party's achievements in the population field have been central to
the first and, even more so, the second pillar of regime legitimacy. Exag-
gerated or not, the party's proud and persistent claims to have averted 400
million births carry the message that without the party's gargantuan birth
project, the economy would have been dragged down by the huge burden
of population growth. Party-led population control, the story goes, greatly
accelerated economic growth and the rise in living standards that has
lifted all boats in China. The population project also helped protect China's natural resources and environment from the destruction that would
have resulted from uncontrolled population growth. These demographic

achievements, the story suggests, have earned the party the continued right to rule.

Population governance has also been crucial to the second pillar of regime legitimacy: the claim to guarantee social and political stability. Here the narrative of population as permanent crisis has been crucial. Not only population growth, but also many other aspects of China's population have been construed as crises requiring strong party solutions. Such looming threats include the rising birth defects and nagging low quality that, according to the official narrative, undermine China's competitiveness; the huge floating population and growing numbers of bachelors that erode political stability; and the rising sex ratio at birth that threatens China's smooth social development. By constantly defining the problems of population as ones of demographic, economic, ecological, social, and political chaos, and by succeeding again and again in averting the catastrophe, the party has been able to claim that it, and it alone, has been responsible for maintaining the sociopolitical stability that allows people to pursue their private work, family, and leisure agendas. From the early reform years, when the narrative of population crisis was first created, the party's apparent success in averting successive crises on the population front has given it powerful grounds for claiming the right to rule.

In these and other ways, the pressing project of "averting the population crisis" has allowed China's reform-era leaders to expand the regime's power around a critical domain: the Chinese people themselves. The political success of this effort should be assessed not by the widespread rural opposition to the one-child policy (which is now declining), but by the society-wide acceptance of the larger project, in particular, the state's account of the "population crisis" and its "necessary solution" of deep intervention in people's bodies and lives. Although the party-state's hegemony has never been total, and its role is now evolving into orchestrating other social forces instead of managing everything by itself, through "resolving the population crisis" the regime has taken charge of the creation and optimization of life itself.

The early 2000s shift in emphasis in population governance from resolving an economic crisis to fostering human development carries major advantages for the party—and the state. Population workers are urged to follow the party's "strategic perspectives" not only of constructing an "all-inclusive, well-off society" and building a "harmonious socialist society," but also of

"having the party benefit the public and the government serve the people";
and having the party "assum[e] responsibility for the future development of
the Chinese nation."[20] The rise of human governance preserves a large role
for the state in managing population in all its dynamic, statistical complexity. For the party, which is set to play the key decision-making role in the
process, the stakes are equally great. Essentially, the shift from population to
human governance is expected to benefit the party by benefitting the Chinese people and the Chinese nation. By addressing people's felt needs—for
old-age support, marriage partners, and so on—and by working increasingly
through individuals' desires, the new directions should directly benefit the
Chinese people, securing their support for the party and its programs. The
new agenda also gives the people a bigger role in their own governance,
(theoretically) deepening popular investment in the system. If the leadership's bet on the centrality of human capital to the twenty-first-century
global economy turns out to be sound, then the attention to "human development" can be also expected to accelerate China's socioeconomic development and emergence as a strong, powerful nation, strengthening the people's
support for the party and ensuring the party's continued role in China's future. In theory, at least, the new regime of population governance is good for
people, party, and state.

Population and the Techno-Scientific State

Population was a crucial site not only for state strengthening, but also for
the construction of a particular kind of state: a techno-scientific state in
which scientific logics and techniques provide both an authoritative basis
for, and a rigorous means of, party rule. The scholarly literature on Chinese
science has lauded the early Deng-era rise of Chinese science and the new
ideal of scientific decision making in which technical experts in the natural
and social sciences provide input into party decision making.[21] The scientific decision making initiated by Deng is seen as a major advance, producing a policy process and product superior to the ideological decision making
of the Mao years.

The political centrality of science and engineering has deepened with
time. In the 2000s, China is a virtual technocracy—ruled by experts—in
which engineers fill every seat on the nine-person Standing Committee of

the Politburo selected in 2002.[22] As we saw earlier, Hu Jintao's political philosophy calls for the construction of a "harmonious society" based on a "scientific concept of development." Hu's scientific development concept sees different fields—economic, environmental, social—as interrelated and seeks to manage them in an integrated way. This thinking embeds the kind of systems engineering approach that we have encountered before. In *What Does China Think?*, international relations scholar Mark Leonard acclaims China's "synergistic approach to various social issues." While cautioning that China is moving in the direction of technocracy rather than liberal democracy, he applauds the country's "deliberative dictatorship" in which big policy decisions are backed up by huge multicentered research projects. The scientific concept of development, he argues, is part of a new Chinese Model of Development that provides a powerful alternative to the Democracy Model purveyed by Washington.[23] Others are less enthusiastic. The China scholar Willy Wo-Lap Lam sees Hu's promotion of science—both a scientific theory of development and a scientific ruling apparatus—as a strategy for perpetuating party rule without adopting democratic reforms. In other words, "science" substitutes for democracy. Hu's belief and fervent hope is that a scientific party wielding scientific governance can "get development right" and earn the right to rule well in the twenty-first century.[24]

Population has been a key site for the construction of the PRC's technoscientific state. In 1979–1980 it became the first arena in which scientific techniques were used in the formulation of party policy. The success of this new kind of mathematical policymaking in producing an apparently scientific strategy to control population growth—the one-child policy—helped secure the leadership's belief in the power of science, especially natural and computer-based science, as a source of solutions to the nation's many problems. Since then "scientific policymaking" has been the political ideal.

Dangers of Politicized Science

Unfortunately, as I have shown elsewhere, the science behind the one-child policy was highly problematic.[25] In the chaotic early years of the Deng administration, the leadership rejected a moderate one-child policy proposal drafted by social scientists in favor of an extreme one-child-for-all policy created by a handful of military scientists who had no knowledge of demography or of the social context in which population dynamics necessarily unfold. The science behind the one-child policy is not really "bogus science," a term some have suggested. According to mathematical demographers who have examined the work that has been translated into English, the technical aspects of the science (projections, cybernetic equations for optimal policy) were sound. Even though at the time there were no solid data on China's population, the long-term projections of China's population under different fertility scenarios provided a plausible sense of future prospects, given certain assumptions. Yet several key aspects of the science behind the one-child policy were deeply problematic. Perhaps most important, the choice of scientific framework was inappropriate for an arena of social policy. The cybernetics of population took no account of social, cultural, and political factors, producing a policy that was out of touch with the realities of rural Chinese society, its intended target, and thus not implementable without massive social and political trauma.

Nevertheless, the strict one-child policy was presented to China's leaders and the public as the only scientific solution to the scientifically defined problem of demographic-environmental-economic crisis. The regime opted for this proposal because it was expressed in highly mathematical terms and thus seemed very scientific, because it was created by researchers associated with the prestigious field of strategic defense science, and because those researchers had the strong support of one of the top natural scientists in the country. This was none other than Qian Xuesen, the cyberneticist and defense scientist we met in Chapter 1. The politicized nature of this "scientific policymaking" process means that for the last thirty years the state has been vigorously enforcing a policy that was unrealistic and problematically scientific at best. It is no wonder that the adverse social and human consequences have been so widespread.

A Larger Voice for Social Scientists

Although genuinely humanistic views on population were forced underground in 1980, conversations with Chinese demographers over many years suggest that, since the late 1980s, more sociologically oriented population scientists have gained a larger voice in the policy and program arena. The key figure supporting their views was Peng Peiyun, a sociologically trained official who assumed leadership of the birth planning commission in 1988. Social scientists have been influential in several key decisions that have worked to ease program enforcement and make it more socially and culturally realistic.[26]

One such decision was the shift in long-term population-plan target. The population target is crucial because it drives policy: the more restrictive the target, the tighter the policy. In 1980, the target for the year 2000 was set at 1.2 billion, an unrealistic goal by any demographic standard. In the mid-1980s, when it became clear that 1.2 billion was unattainable, the goal was quietly changed to "about 1.2 billion"—still unrealizable. When Peng assumed control of the birth planning commission, she announced that whatever its level, the nation's population target must be achievable. During the Seventh Five-Year Plan (1986–1990), few localities had fulfilled their population plans. In 1990, social scientists involved in creating the ten-year population plan for the 1990s quietly persuaded Minister Peng that the year-2000 target must be changed to 1.3 billion. Their calculations assumed not one but two children per couple—a more manageable goal. Peng took the proposal to the Politburo, the nation's highest decision-making body, and gained approval. Given the leadership's historically uncompromising approach to population control, this was an extraordinary achievement.[27]

Social scientists were also instrumental in making the rising sex ratio at birth a governmental concern. In the 1980s the possibility that a tough one-child policy might lead peasants to get rid of their infant daughters and raise the sex ratio among newborns was a taboo topic: population specialists were not allowed to study it and editors were forbidden to publish on it. Yet later in that decade, Chinese demographers analyzing survey data discovered an alarming rise in the sex ratio at birth and quietly shared the information with Minister Peng. Peng arranged a meeting between the demographers and China's top leaders in 1993. Finally persuaded about the urgency of the problem, in 1993 officials began to issue circulars forbidding the use of ultrasound to detect fetal sex and the use of abortion to eliminate female fetuses.[28] The policy on fertility was not eased, but from that point on the sex ratio would be a focus of growing policy concern.

Social scientists also had a hand in the reorientation of the birth program in the mid- to late 1990s away from exclusive emphasis on demographic control toward greater concern for reproductive health. Behind this critical move was a team of two specialists, Peng's right-hand man, a trained engineer tasked with "guaranteeing the bottom line"—that is, keeping the population numbers within target—and a social demographer concerned about the human costs of the one-child policy. I talked to both of them in 1993 and again in 1999. Arguing that "behind the numbers are thousands upon thousands of families" *(shuhou you yiwan hu),* the social scientist persuaded the program's target cop that the human costs of drastic policy enforcement were severe enough to mandate a softening of enforcement. These conversations were a major force behind the "two transformations" ushering in a reform of work methods (though not of the policy or plan).[29]

In the early twenty-first century, the cyberneticists retain a big behind-the-scenes influence on China's birth policy (see Chapter 1). Yet the voice of social scientists is growing louder. Today, many in Beijing are arguing for the gradual relaxation of the one-child policy, using a variety of social scientific data and arguments to make the case. By tallying up the frightening future social, demographic, and economic costs of retaining that troubling policy, and by assessing the demographic achievements of various two-child policy experiments, for example, they have been seeking to create momentum for policy change.[30] Drawing on this research, in 2004 a group of social scientists presented a report and proposal for policy change to the birth commission. It was not accepted. In January 2009 they presented another report, this time bypassing the population commission and delivering their ideas directly to China's leaders.

Whatever the outcome of that initiative, the political struggles over the one-child policy going on in Beijing today are rooted in part in contests between social and natural scientists for the decisive voice on the fate of the one-child policy (or, more accurately, for the ear of supportive factions within the decision-making elite). Current shifts in China's top leadership might give greater scope to social scientific perspectives in coming years. Although China remains a technocracy, with engineers dominating the apex of the political system, just below this level the number of officials schooled in economics and management is growing rapidly. Of roughly sixty provincial leaders studied in 2005, ten had degrees in engineering and thirteen had degrees in economics. Most of the new provincial heads appointed at the 2004 Fourth Plenum of the 16th Central Committee have been educated in economics and management.[31] Li Bin, appointed minister-in-charge of the Population and Birth Planning Commission in March 2008, has a doctorate in economics.[32] Although the fields of economics and management may pay less attention to the human subject than the less quantitative social sciences, this incoming cohort of leaders can be expected to give more serious consideration to the social, cultural, and economic factors that argue for abandoning the one-child policy at the soonest possible time.

Creating a Global China: The Quest for Global Good Citizenship

From the early Deng years, population has been central to the social and economic agendas of a globalizing regime. Under the policy of "reform and opening up," from the late 1970s the makers of China's population project have energetically sought out foreign advice, concepts, and technology, sinifying and employing them wherever useful. They have also actively welcomed the (constructive) participation of foreign specialists and organizations in the birth program. The aim has been to incorporate best international practice into China's population-and-reproduction work—wherever that also advanced Chinese goals—demonstrating China's identity as a modern, advanced nation and a responsible actor in the world community.

As a result, China's policy and program bear strong if selective traces of foreign ideas. As we saw earlier, foreign scientific ideas and techniques were instrumental in the making of the one-child policy. International approaches to policy implementation and program management have been important sources of programmatic reform since around the mid-1990s. That decade's emphasis on "women's reproductive health," "informed choice," and "quality of care," for example, was shaped in good part by China's effort to conform to new international norms of population-management-as-reproductive-health adopted at the 1994 Cairo Conference on Population and Development. The move to make family planning more women-friendly and human-centered was influenced by the 1993 Vienna Conference on Human Rights and the 1995 Fourth World Women's Conference in Beijing. The late 1990s and early 2000s embrace of "scientific management" and "human-centered" frameworks for program management and evaluation also drew on notions of best practice in the international community.

China's multifaceted project on population and reproduction has not only connected its population field to transnational networks of demographers and family planning specialists; it has also actively contributed to China's global ascent. The population project was to facilitate the nation's rise in three ways: socially, by fostering a society standardized to the modern norm; economically, by speeding the achievement of world-class per-capita income levels; and ethically, by demonstrating China's emergence as a responsible and ethical member of the world community of nations. How did things turn out? Did population help transform China into a global power? What else did it accomplish at the same time? I examined the project of social globalization in the last chapter. Here I consider the ethical agenda before turning to the economic goal and a more contemporary objective of boosting China's "comprehensive national power."

An Ethical and Responsible Nation: The Dream

To much of the world, China's compulsory birth policy represents one of the world's most blatant violations of the international ethical norm that the number of children a couple has should be freely chosen. To its makers in China, however, the one-child project was driven by a profoundly ethical agenda, one they thought would gain worldwide approbation. Discussions around the country in the mid-1980s suggest that, to these early reform-era population leaders, population governance presented an extraordinary opportunity to demonstrate China's keen sense of responsibility toward the world and its embrace of an ethics of global-mindedness. At that time China had the world's largest population and it was growing rapidly. By taking decisive charge of Chinese population growth, they figured, the PRC could lower the population growth rate of the entire world, benefitting humanity at large. By relying not on force but on Mao's much touted method of propaganda-and-education to change childbearing desires, the PRC would also demonstrate the continued value of socialism in an increasingly capitalist world. For its efforts, China would earn worldwide respect.

Such hopes were soon dashed, however. As we saw in the last chapter, the ideal of "state guidance, mass voluntarism" turned out to be achievable only in the cities, where the party maintained tight control over people's lives. In the countryside, the early 1980s dismantling of the collectives, combined with other reforms, enabled rural couples to defy party authority and resist the one-child rule. The birth planning establishment reacted by using physical force against people and property. Campaign-style hard birth planning remained the dominant mode of enforcing the birth policy into the early 1990s.

In the early 1980s, before news of these forceful measures reached the outside world, China was widely praised for finally adopting a strong policy to slow the growth of its gigantic population, then almost one-quarter of the world's total. In 1982, international observers lauded the nation's success in conducting its first modern census. In 1983, the UN awarded Qian Xinzhong, the PRC birth minister, together with Indian Prime Minister Indira Gandhi, the first UN Population Award "for their vision and foresight in responding to the formidable challenge of controlling population growth."[33] In his speech, the Secretary-General of the UN, Javier-Perez de Cuellar, described "the paramount urgency" of the population problem. "If rapid population growth in the developing nations is left unchecked," he warned, "it will . . . undermine all efforts for economic and social development and could easily lead to widespread depletion of each nation's basic resources." The United Nations "deeply appreciat[es how these two] Governments have marshalled the resources necessary to implement population policies on a massive scale."[34] Not surprisingly, the Chinese thought the world community shared their vision of China's population growth as an urgent problem demanding drastic response.

Unwelcome Reactions

It did not take long for them to learn otherwise. As we saw in Chapter 1, by the mid-1980s the Western media had begun to document widespread human rights abuses in the Chinese birth program. Over the next decade, many Westerners came to associate the Chinese program with news photos and stories of such travesties as baby girls being drowned in wells, pregnant rural women fleeing the birth control squad, and doctors being forced to perform late-term abortions despite threats to women's health. Western public opinion on China's birth program and policy turned harshly critical.

By the mid-1980s, the issue of coercion in the PRC program had become the *cause célèbre* of social conservatives in the United States with anti-abortion agendas (the details are in the first chapter). Under their influence, the issue became a hot topic in American domestic politics and U.S. policy toward China. Responding to these favored constituents, between 1986 and 1992 the U.S. administrations of Ronald Reagan (1981–1989) and George H. W. Bush (1989–1993) withheld all contributions to the United Nations Population Fund (UNFPA) approved by Congress on the grounds that the Fund "supports or participates in the management of a program of coerced abortion or involuntary sterilization."[35] Because the decision on funding required an annual deliberation (by the Administrator of U.S. Agency for International Development) on whether the Chinese program remained co-ercive, every spring the latest stories of state coercion and peasant resistance were publicized and heatedly debated on Capitol Hill, keeping the issue alive in the political and public imagination. In 1993 President Bill Clinton restored the UN agency's funding on the condition that no U.S. funds be used in China until 1999. In that year, Congress, worried about a new UN-FPA program in China, banned contributions to the agency. For 2000 and 2001, Congress allocated funds, but required that they be reduced by the amount that UNFPA spent in China. In mid-2002 the George W. Bush ad-ministration again held back the entire American contribution to the UN-FPA, and did so every year for the next six years. In March 2009, President Barack Obama signed legislation paving the way for the release of $50 mil-lion in U.S. funds for the UN agency, bringing to an end this long and diffi-cult chapter in U.S.–China relations.[36]

While these debates over UNFPA funding were going on, the coercion narrative became embedded in U.S. immigration law. The Immigration and Nationality Act of 1996 amended the definition of "refugee" to grant politi-cal asylum to foreigners who could show legitimate worry about coercive birth control surgery. While not naming China, this provision clearly was introduced with China in mind, and it has given rise to a surge of applica-tions for asylum from Chinese citizens claiming past persecution or fear of persecution under the one-child policy.[37] Those whose applications have been denied have sometimes taken their cases to courts of law and, at times, of American public opinion. The legalization of these cases has given the is-sue of coercion in the Chinese program a new lease on life.

In the early 1980s, the Chinese were totally unprepared for such hostile reactions. Western demographers invited to lecture in China in the early reform years found that the Chinese population community, which had had little contact with the outside world for decades, was ill prepared to respond to the coercion critique.[38] Many of the Chinese planners and specialists I talked to in the mid-1980s were genuinely mystified by the about-face exhibited by the international population community. The PRC's official response to the criticism of foreign journalists and politicians has been to reject the accusations. Where an official Chinese investigation lent support to the charges, the problems were blamed on low-quality local cadres. Beneath the indignation, however, the reports of coercion have certainly been cause for national shame. As we have seen, China's self-identity, especially in the post-Mao years, has been based on the notion that the party uses education—not force—to induce social and demographic change.

Difficult though they have been to accept, the media critiques have helped China's population officials to see, probably for the first time, the human rights problems in the uncompromising approach of the Deng years. In the late 1990s I was invited to speak to several groups of top birth officials attending the Advanced Leadership Program seminar in Princeton, New Jersey, about the coercion narratives in the *New York Times* and *Washington Post*.[39] My detailed analyses of the methods by which the narratives were constructed and the values they purveyed produced reactions of shock and chagrin, as officials who had seen the program's heavy-handed measures as necessary to avert a national crisis—or just business-as-usual—were forced to re-see them through an international human rights lens. Chinese officials have also been open to constructive (but not hostile) forms of scholarly critique, especially those that acknowledge improvements the program has made so far. These critiques have provided intellectual resources for those seeking to reform the program and relax the one-child policy. Conversations over many years suggest that over time the media exposés, along with the scholarly critiques, have quietly encouraged positive change.

Today the climate of opinion surrounding the Chinese program is quite different. One reason, undoubtedly, is that in the wake of the Cairo process and the widespread shift from demographic control to women- and health-oriented programs, the critique of coercive population control has lost much of its salience. As fertility rates have fallen around the world, the

international population community has turned its attention to other issues, including reproductive health and HIV/AIDS. In China, too, things
have changed. At the national level, China has substantially reformed its
birth planning program and abandoned coercive campaigns in favor of
more indirect, self-fostering techniques of governance. In all but the poorest regions, childbearing preferences have fallen to what may be historic
lows, making coercive practices less necessary. In the early 2000s, the PRC
is viewed as a responsible state whose success in reducing its own population growth rates has greatly benefitted the world community. A back-of-
the-envelope calculation suggests that during the four decades 1960/1965
to 2000/2005, China's success in lowering its own population growth increased the world fertility decline by 7 percent (from 39 to 46 percent),
while raising the worldwide reduction in population growth 8 percent
(from 30 to 38 percent). Chinese demographers are rightly proud of their
country's contributions to accelerating the global demographic transition
and to ensuring that the world's population will likely peak at around 10
billion.[40] On these fronts, the birth program—together with exceptionally
rapid economic growth—have accomplished what Chinese development
planners had hoped for.

Yet even today, praise from the international community is subdued, for
in the minds of many the means used to reduce fertility have been as important as the ends. One step that has earned China (cautiously) positive press
is the introduction, in the mid-1990s, of a wide range of women-centered,
health-oriented reforms. Although the Chinese reforms are not feminist in
the sense of giving women power to shape their own reproductive lives, they
represent a distinct improvement. As efforts to improve health and quality
of care develop, as experiments in more voluntary family planning spread
from the richer to the poorer areas, and as the shift from population to social policy and human development takes on more concrete meanings, the
global image of the Chinese population-and-birth program should become
even more positive.

Yet ethical concerns persist, and for good reasons. One is that the one-
child-with-exceptions policy is still in place. Another is that violations of
human rights and violent struggles over the birth policy still occur in some
areas, though much more rarely now than in the past. Millennial China is
marked by glaring gaps between rich and poor groups, advanced and back-

ward regions, privileged and underprivileged ethnicities. In many poor groups and areas, people continue to resent and resist the one-child-with-exceptions policy. An increasingly complex society keeps throwing up new ways to get around the one-child rule. Some of those methods are peaceful. In rural Henan, for example, one can find villages full of families with twins and triplets and even quintuplets. Their mothers beat the system by taking fertility drugs.[41] In other areas the protests are more violent. In early 2007, for example, a vicious crackdown on births in the southwestern region of Guangxi led to four days of rioting.[42] In a harsh, two-month campaign, local officials had forced pregnant women without birth permits to undergo abortion, imposed mandatory health checks, levied exorbitant fines and, when people refused to pony up, confiscated their valuables or even demolished their homes. Incensed at the local officials' violation of Central policy, several thousand villagers upended official vehicles, destroyed documents, and sacked and burned government offices. The Guangxi riot was one of the largest episodes of violent protest over birth planning in recent years. The persistence of such convulsions tells us that side by side with the new biopolitical regime of birth planning that works through individual desires, there exist pockets of the old regime that relies on force. Unlike the cities, which are generally stable and prosperous, large parts of rural China, especially in the central, western, and mountainous parts of the country, have been left behind by the economic boom. In some of these areas, Beijing rules do not apply and local officials continue to do business by the old, Maoist ways. The new regime is spreading, but it has not replaced the old; instead, new coexists with old in uneasy tension.

Such infringements of human rights are not the only issues of ethical concern; so, too, are the adverse social legacies of the birth planning program. One, of course, is the rising sex ratio at birth. Whether through killing, abandonment, or sex-selective abortion, the systematic elimination of girls from China's population has been deeply troubling. If the tens of millions of poor rural men who cannot find brides react in severely antisocial ways (by becoming violent, for example, or defying fundamental moral codes), ethical concerns about the distorted gender regime will deepen. In the years ahead, the second damaging social structural consequence of the birth program—the accelerated aging of China's population—will pose another set of ethical problems. Hundreds of millions of Chinese lacking state and family forms of social security would tarnish China's cherished image of itself as a nation that takes exemplary care of its elderly citizens.

Opportunities to Gain "Soft Power"

Today, there is much talk in Beijing about "soft power." By a nation's soft power, China's intellectuals and leaders mean its ability to influence the thinking and governmental approaches of other nations. This ability to influence others rests on the attractiveness and international legitimacy of a nation's culture and ideas.[43] As China's propaganda director put it, "In this modern era, who[ever] gains the advanced communication skills . . . and whose culture and value[s are] more widely spread, is able to more effectively influence the world."[44] Political scientist David M. Lampton calls this ability "ideational power," to distinguish it from economic and coercive power.[45] In the Chinese view, the United States has long maintained a monopoly on soft power, which it has used to diminish the PRC's achievements in the international arena. Western news organizations, for example, have often portrayed the PRC in what the Chinese consider unflattering ways. Chinese elites believe that possessing soft power (as well as "hard power," discussed just below) is essential to being a great power. In what Kurlantzick calls a "charm offensive," China's leaders are seeking to strengthen China's soft power, in order to make China a respected and, in time, increasingly influential nation in world affairs.[46]

Although Chinese intellectuals appear to have paid little attention to the population sector, the construction and wide dissemination of the coercion narrative about China's population program provides a striking example of how the opinion makers in the United States (government, public officials, and media) have used the discursive dimension of America's soft power to China's detriment. While the narrative appropriately highlights the violation of individual human rights in the birth program, with its exclusive emphasis on state coercion and state–society struggle, it provides no way to acknowledge the positive accomplishments program managers have achieved, including their relatively successful efforts over the past decade to remove abusive practices and gradually bring the program into line with accepted international practice. With its reforms of the birth program and efforts to foster south-to-south cooperation in family planning, China's population establishment has been working hard to improve its international legitimacy and image.

There is another, much more dramatic and effective step China's leaders could take to boost China's soft power: they could abandon the one-child policy. The first move would be to revise the official fertility rate. To keep the "alarm bell ringing," as they put it, China's officials have continued to claim a fertility rate of 1.8, when the real rate, according to a broad scholarly consensus, is around 1.5 to 1.6. Using the higher fertility level, official China worries about a fertility rebound that might follow a policy liberalization. Many Chinese demographers, however, believe that softening the policy would be demographically almost neutral.[47] Ethnographic research on changing fertility desires suggests the same conclusion.[48] Even today, the strict one-child rule applies only to about one-third of the population.[49] Although shifting to a two-child policy (the most plausible alternative) would not immediately even out the sex ratio at birth, it should improve the lot of infant girls by discouraging many couples from getting rid of their female fetuses and abandoning their baby daughters. It would also eliminate the conflict between the official goal of gender equality and a fertility policy that constrains women to abort their unborn daughters. Over the longer run, dropping the one-child policy would also slow the rise in the bachelor population and ease the problem of aging-without-social-security.

Beyond this major step, population leaders could also soften the sanctions against officials who exceed the birth limits. Since around 1990, officials at any level whose domains have exceeded the birth targets have been subject to severe sanctions, including demotion, salary reductions, and removal from office. These harsh punishments have had countless adverse effects, including the use of coercion against the people and falsification of population numbers, which in turn has undermined the quality of China's population data.[50] Because of the symbolic importance of the birth policy and program, which for some thirty years have stood for China's open disregard of its people's reproductive rights, taking these steps would have major symbolic significance, signaling China's move beyond coercive to ideational power. By making this courageous move, China's leaders could signal to the world that in this key area of social and human governance, a globally ascending China is a responsible stakeholder not only demographically, but also ethically, and has fully accepted the international norm that reproductive programs be gender-equitable and people-centered. Changing the policy might open the space for the past accomplishments of the program and current positive directions to gain international recognition and, more generally, for Chinese social policy ideas and practices to be accorded the legitimacy and admiration the Chinese have long believed they deserve.

Population and China's Comprehensive National Power

In the late 1970s and early 1980s, when China was driven by an economy-first mentality, economic goals dominated the choice of population policy: adopting the one-child policy was deemed the surest, fastest way to boost per capita living standards and, in turn, transform China into an economic powerhouse. Today China no longer measures its global greatness in simple economic terms such as the gross domestic product. Since the mid-1980s, Chinese thinkers have developed a broad-based measure of national power, known as "comprehensive national power" (*zonghe guoli*, or CNP), that includes security, political, economic, ethical, and population/social factors. This concept reflects serious concerns about the international security environment and widely shared desires to make China a rich and powerful nation in charge of its own destiny.[51] The PRC routinely measures itself against only a handful of other big and/or important countries: the two Asian powers India and Japan, Russia, and, of course, the United States. As two top Chinese researchers put it, these four countries are "closely associated with China's national interests and geopolitical strategy."[52]

Regime leaders and intellectuals believe that the economic globalization of recent decades has been accelerating the competition among nations, and especially among the big powers. To keep from falling behind, China must respond with massive and unrelenting efforts to boost its own power in the international sphere. There appears to be a broad, implicit consensus among ruling and intellectual elites on a national "grand strategy" for the next twenty years.[53] Recognizing that Washington will remain dominant until at least 2015–2020, Beijing's strategy is to get along with Washington while quietly though relentlessly building up the nation's military, economic, and ideational power. While focusing its energies over the next decade on internal growth and stability, the overall goal is to boost China's CNP, making the PRC an ever more important and influential actor on the world stage. To counter fears, especially in the United States, that a rising China poses a threat to the existing world order, the regime depicts this process as China's "peaceful rise" *(heping jueqi)* and "peaceful development" *(heping fazhan)*, and works hard to project China's "soft-power nation" image.[54]

The CNP is distinctive (and putatively scientific) in that it enables Chinese researchers to quantitatively assess China's power relative to other actors by combining a variety of quantified indices into a single number. It also allows them to see how much each factor has contributed to China's CNP to date, and how each might be manipulated through public policy to ensure an optimal national power and security environment in the future. CNP thus provides a guide to China's changing global position in the past and a map for future action. Like all such measures, including similar measures developed abroad, this one suffers from methodological difficulties, including problems of measurement, data accuracy, and data comparability.[55] Whatever the CNP's scientific limitations—and perhaps scientistic pretensions—it is critical to understand, because it figures importantly in the strategic calculations and policy thinking of political and intellectual leaders in Beijing. Indeed, raising the CNP is the ultimate goal of much of Chinese development and international relations policy. Increasing China's CNP is now an explicit objective of China's population and human development strategy, legitimizing efforts to keep population growth down and to continue raising health, education, and other dimensions of population quality. So, let us forego critically deconstructing the concept and instead examine how it actually figures in policy debates in Beijing.

Population/Human Capital and China's Global Greatness

Population occupies a prominent place in these assessments of China's power. Although there are various models and formulae, with different indicators and weights, virtually all recognize the existence of two kinds of power. Soft power, discussed just above, is generally assessed qualitatively. Hard power, which is closer to conventional notions of national power, is measured quantitatively. Hard power, which includes military might and economic prowess, accords a significant place to population factors. In the model of "tangible strategic resources" developed by the influential Beijing-based scholars Hu Angang and Men Honghua, there are eight main factors and twenty-three indicators. The eight main factors are: economic resources (GDP), human capital (working-age population and education), natural resources, capital resources, knowledge and technology resources, government resources, military resources, and international resources. The results of Hu and Men's research, published in 2002 and updated in 2007, are shown in Table 6.

Table 6 (Panel B) shows changes in CNP between 1980 and 2003. This table compares China with the four other big countries against which it measures itself. Although the United States remains the global superpower, with a total CNP of 22.274 in 2003, between 1980 and 2003 China's CNP increased the most, from 4.736 to 9.991, for a total gain of 5.255 (in contrast to the U.S.'s net loss of .211 point).[56] China has risen from

Table 6   Comprehensive National Power: China and Its Benchmark Countries

A. Human Capital as Percentage of World Total

	1980	1998	Change, 1980–1998
China	17.60	24.0	+6.4
India	8.40	12.3	+3.9
Japan	4.36	3.27	−1.09
Russia	5.69	4.06	−1.63
United States	11.6	8.6	−3.0
Five in World Total	47.7	52.2	+.45

B. Comprehensive National Power

	1980	2003	Change, 1980–2003
China	4.736	9.991	+5.255
India	3.376	4.868	+1.492
Japan	6.037	6.998	+.961
Russia	—	2.934	—
United States	22.485	22.274	−.211
Total, Five Countries		47.065	—

Source: 1980 figures from Hu Angang and Men Honghua, "The Rise of Modern China: Comprehensive National Power and Grand Strategy," *Strategy and Management* (2002), Table 12 (in Chinese); 2003 figures from Lampton, *Three Faces of Chinese Power: Might, Money, and Minds* (Berkeley: University of California Press, 2008), p. 23.

fourth position in 1980 (behind the United States, Japan, and Russia) to become the second world power. And the gap between China and the United States has narrowed: in 1980 the United States had 4.7 times the CNP of China; by 2003 the American advantage had shrunk to 2.2 times. Other studies using slightly different computational methods reach similar conclusions.

What accounts for the dramatic rise in Chinese power? Let us look again at the research of Hu and Men. Of the eight factors making up hard power, improvements in the economy and in human capital/population accounted for the greatest part of the overall increase in China's CNP. Table 6 (Panel A) also shows changes in human capital in these five nations, measured as the proportion of working age people (those 15–64 years of age) in the world's total and the average years of schooling. Here we find that, between 1980 and 1999, China's share of total global human capital grew from 17.6 to 24 percent, an increase of 6.4 percent. India's share of the world's human capital also rose, from 8.4 to 12.3 percent, a rise of 3.9 percent. Meantime, the share of global human capital possessed by the other three countries fell by 1 to 3 percent. The United States lost 3 percentage points. As Hu and Men put it, "China has become a No. 1 big power in terms of population but also in terms of total human capital. This is the biggest advantage in its national strategic resources."[57]

These figures help explain China's improving overall CNP. Between 1980 and 1998, the extraordinary improvement in economic performance (the GDP) contributed 46.4 percent to the rise in the CNP, while improvements in human capital made up 21 percent. Of that latter, the rise in educational level (related to the quality project on population) accounted for 54.8 percent, while the change in working-age population (related to the quantity project on fertility decline) contributed 45.2 percent. Both quantity control and quality enhancement thus contributed to the dramatic improvement in China's national prowess.

Changes in the fertility level and thus age structure contributed not only directly to measures of human capital, they also contributed indirectly, through their effects on the growth in the GDP. In the 1980s and 1990s China's economy spurted, growing at an average annual rate of 9 percent. Research by demographers suggests that the rapid fertility decline of the Deng era enabled China to jump through a once-in-history window of developmental opportunity. Wang Feng and Andrew Mason have calculated that 15 percent of China's economic growth between 1982 and 2000 can be attributed to a so-called "demographic dividend" to economic development from a temporary surplus of productive adults.[58] By around 2000, the age-structure gains began to slow. If we extend the end date to 2013, the dividend (from 1982–2013) accounts for a more modest 4 percent of the increase in output per capita. From here on, the demographic impact on the economy begins to turn negative. The burden of a rapidly aging population is likely to slow if not jeopardize China's growth in the future.[59]

A key question, of course, is how much of the fertility decline is due to the birth program. Program officials routinely claim to have averted 400 million births. Without the program, they assert, China's population would be not 1.3, but 1.7 billion. There can be no doubt that the birth program contributed importantly to the fall in Chinese fertility. Although impossible to measure precisely, one of its major contributions may have lain in the insistent propaganda and education that helped define the one-child family as a marker of the modern couple and modern person. China's people were very receptive to this message, in part because it was supported by wider changes in the society and economy. The harsh measures put in place to deter "excess" childbearing, especially since the early 1980s, also contributed in some unmeasurable way to the drop in Chinese fertility to historic lows.

Nonetheless, official claims greatly exaggerate the impact of the program on the declines in fertility and population growth. If we consider the economics and culture of family formation, it is clear that, especially since the early 1990s, when the pace of marketization accelerated, the erosion of the traditional family and changes in child economics have been at least as fundamental as, if not more fundamental than, program efforts. A large body of anthropological research, some of which I discussed in the last chapter, shows that major transitions in rural family life—the rise in the costs of child rearing, the erosion of filial obligations, the decline in the intergenerational exchange system, and the growing importance of women to the family economy, for example—have helped to fuel the decline in family size preferences. The big picture is that since the early 1990s, the state's role in managing fertility and population size has declined, while individuals and couples are playing ever-larger roles in the governance of their own childbearing and rearing. The state's claim to have averted 400 million births should be taken with a large grain of salt.

Population/Human Governance in China's Future

Of course, these numbers on CNP should not be taken very seriously. It does not matter much if the contribution of population to China's overall power is 21 percent or 26 percent or 31 percent. What should be taken seriously is that population change has made a very substantial contribution to the overall rise in China's national prowess, and Chinese intellectuals, decision makers, and the people themselves are well aware of that.

What matters more is what conclusions China's policymakers draw from numbers such as these and what directions they map out for future social policy. As we saw earlier, China's population work is currently undergoing a big shift that is realigning it with the new emphasis on overarching national power. Equally important, population is being equated with human capital and redefined as a newly positive factor in China's increasingly knowledge-based development and global ascent. The aim of the Eleventh Five-Year Plan (2006–2010) is to use the scientific concept of development to promote all-round human development. The new plan stresses people's development rather than simply measures of material increase such as the GDP. From now on, growth is to be considered only the means of development, not its end. The larger aim is to transform population, for decades deemed a major obstacle to China's modernization, into a positive resource for advance. Population is to be treated as an asset; a form of human capital that will improve citizen health and education, boost China's sustainable social and economic development, reduce absolute poverty, and enhance the nation's comprehensive national power, ensuring its continued rise in international power rankings. What this means concretely is that there will be increased investment in population quality, or human capital, in all its manifest forms—health, education, genetics, ethics, and so on.[60] All indications are that optimizing China's people will remain a key objective of state investment and administration, and vital politics—however it plays out in China's society—will remain a central arena of governance for a long time to come.

Notes

1. From Population to Human Governance

1. Data from 2007, United Nations Population Fund, *State of World Population 2007*, Table on Demographic, Social and Economic Indicators, pp. 90–93, www. unfpa.org (accessed 2/13/08).

2. In the late 1990s, 35.4 percent of China's population lived in regions with a strict one-child policy; 53.6 percent lived in areas with a 1.5-child policy, 9.7 percent lived in provinces with a two-child policy, while 1.3 percent lived in regions where 3 children were allowed. Gu Baochang, Wang Feng, Guo Zhigang, and Zhang Erli, "China's Local and National Fertility Policies at the End of the Twentieth Century," *Population and Development Review* 33 (2007), pp. 129–147.

3. "China Won't Waver in Family Planning Policy: Official," *Xinhua News,* March 6, 2008, www.wsichina.org (accessed 3/8/08). See also Jim Yardley, "China Says One-Child Policy Will Stay for at Least Another Decade," *New York Times,* March 11, 2008, p. A10.

A word on terminology. China's core project on population is not "family planning," a liberal project in which families plan their own childbearing, but an authoritarian project in which the state plans the births of couples countrywide and tries to persuade them to comply. In most places I translate the Chinese term *jihua shengyu* as (state) birth planning. Where convention demands the use of "family planning," I use that term instead. After twenty years of harsh state birth planning, in the 2000s the Chinese program is gradually evolving into a hybrid entity that mixes elements from the two approaches to population governance. I discuss these changes in the next chapter.

4. David Barboza, "1 Plus 1: Shanghai Tweaks Child Rules," *New York Times,* July 25, 2009, www.nytimes.com (accessed 7/31/09).

5. Variations of this narrative can be found in Judith Banister's *China's Changing Population* (Stanford: Stanford University Press, 1987), and Thomas Scharping's *Birth Control in China 1949–2000: Population Policy and Demographic Development* (London: Curzon, 2003). Both studies, by demographers (Scharping is also a political scientist), are major contributions to our understanding of the

birth program and its demographic consequences. Political scientist Tyrene White's incisive account of China's mobilizational-campaign approach to birth planning gives central place to the dynamic of state power and rural resistance. See her *China's Longest Campaign: Birth Planning in the People's Republic, 1949–2005* (Ithaca, NY: Cornell University Press, 2006).

6. Matthew Connelly, *Fatal Misconception: The Struggle to Control World Population* (Cambridge, MA: Harvard University Press, 2008), esp. pp. 327–364.

7. The following discussion is based largely on Barbara B. Crane and Jason L. Finkle, "The United States, China, and the United Nations Population Fund: Dynamics of US Policymaking," *Population and Development Review* 15 (1989), pp. 23–59.

8. These items were carried in the *Post* on January 8–10, 1985.

9. Washington, DC: American Enterprise Institute Press, 1989. Aird's work relied on an older, totalitarian model of the Chinese state and drew its material exclusively from the Chinese media, neglecting its propagandistic and political functions.

10. Other influential, quasi-scholarly voices—especially those of Judith Banister at the U.S. Census Bureau and Stephen Mosher, a one-time graduate student in Chinese studies who had observed coercion in practice in China—combined research with moralism in a potent mix that had great appeal to members of the New Right.

11. John S. Aird, *Slaughter of the Innocents: Coercive Birth Control in China* (Washington, DC: American Enterprise Institute Press, 1989), pp. 108–109. See also his report prepared for the Senate Foreign Affairs Committee, "Coercion in Family Planning: Causes, Methods, and Consequences," available in "Foreign Relations Authorization Act, Fiscal Years 1986 and 1987," *Congressional Record—Senate,* June 7, 1985 (Washington, DC: Government Printing Office), pp. S7775–S7788.

12. Statement at hearing on the Impact of the Olympics on Human Rights in China, February 27, 2008, posted on the Web site of the Congressional-Executive Commission on China, http://cecc.gov (accessed 3/18/09).

13. Lucy Hornby, "China May Scrap One-Child Policy, Official Says," Reuters, February 28, 2008, www.reuters.com (accessed 2/28/08).

14. *Xinhua News,* March 6, 2008.

15. Key texts include Michel Foucault, *History of Sexuality: An Introduction, Volume I* (New York: Vintage, 1978); *Security, Territory, Population: Lectures at the Collège de France 1977–1978* (New York: Palgrave Macmillan, 2007), trans. by Graham Burchell; *The Birth of Biopolitics: Lectures at the Collège de France 1978–1979* (New York: Palgrave Macmillan, 2008), trans. by Graham Burchell. Classic studies of governmentality include Graham Burchell, Colin Gordon, and Peter Miller, eds., *The Foucault Effect: Studies in Governmentality* (Chicago:

University of Chicago Press, 1991); Michell Dean, *Governmentality: Power and Rule in Modern Society* (London: Sage, 1999), and Nikolas Rose, *Powers of Freedom: Reframing Political Thought* (Cambridge, UK: Cambridge University Press, 1999).

16. See, for example, Matthew Kohrman, *Bodies of Difference: Experiences of Disability and Institutional Advocacy in the Making of Modern China* (Berkeley: University of California Press, 2005); Nancy N. Chen, "Consuming Medicine and Biotechnology in China," in Li Zhang and Aihwa Ong, eds., *Privatizing China: Socialism from Afar* (Ithaca, NY: Cornell University Press, 2008), pp. 123–132; Aihwa Ong and Nancy N. Chen, eds., *Asian Biotechnology: Population, Security, and Nation* (Durham, NC: Duke University Press, 2009).

17. For Mitchell Dean, this refers to the growth and elaboration of the rationalities and techniques of government within the state. See his *Governmentality: Power and Rule in Modern Society* (London: Sage, 1989), pp. 106–108.

18. The population crisis could only be virtual because officially China remained a Marxian state ideologically opposed to the heresies of Malthus and his neo-Malthusian followers, both of which saw population growth as outstripping the growth of economic resources and thus requiring strong external control.

19. On China's national narrative and its reconstruction in the reform era, see Alan R. Kluver, *Legitimating the Chinese Economic Reforms: A Rhetoric of Myth and Orthodoxy* (Albany: State University of New York Press, 1996).

20. Carl J. Dahlman and Jean-Eric Aubert, *China and the Knowledge Economy: Seizing the 21st Century* (Washington, DC: World Bank, 2001), p. 4.

21. Dahlman and Aubert, *China and the Knowledge Economy*, p. 69.

22. On overall trends in China's reform strategy in the 2000s, see Willy Wo-Lap Lam, *Chinese Politics in the Hu Jintao Era: New Leaders, New Challenges* (Armonk, NY: M. E. Sharpe, 2006); John Wong and Lai Hongyi, eds., *China into the Hu-Wen Era: Policy Initiatives and Challenges* (Hackensack, NJ: World Scientific, 2006); and Tun-jen Cheng, Jacques deLisle, and Deborah Brown, eds., *China under Hu Jintao: Opportunities, Dangers, and Dilemmas* (Hackensack, NJ: World Scientific, 2006).

23. Information on the Eleventh Five-Year Plan can be found at several government Web sites, including www.china.org and ndrc.gov.cn. "Decision of the Central Committee of the Communist Party of China and the State Council on Fully Enhancing [the] Population and Family Planning Program and Comprehensively Addressing Population Issues," January 22, 2007, at www.npfpc.gov.cn (accessed 3/23/07). All page numbers given below refer to location in this English-language text. The following discussion is based primarily on these items.

24. Decision, p. 1.

25. Decision, p. 2

26. Edwin A. Winckler, "Maximizing the Impact of Cairo on China," in Wendy Chavkin and Ellen Chesler, eds., *Where Human Rights Begin: Essays on Health, Sexuality, and Women, Ten Years after Vienna, Cairo, and Beijing* (Piscataway, NJ: Rutgers University Press); Joan Kaufman, Zhang Erli, and Xie Zhenming, "Quality of Care in China: Scaling Up a Pilot Project into a National Reform Program," *Studies in Family Planning* 37 (2006), pp. 17–28. For a broad overview of the reforms introduced in the 1990s, see Susan Greenhalgh and Edwin A. Winckler, *Governing China's Population: From Leninist to Neoliberal Biopolitics* (Stanford: Stanford University Press, 2005), chapter 5.

27. On the priority of social governance during the Hu–Wen administration, see Willy Wo-Lap Lam, *Chinese Politics in the Hu Jintao Era,* esp. chapter 3; Wong and Lai, eds., *China into the Hu-Wen Era,* chapters 12–17.

28. "Decision of the CPC Central Committee and the State Council on Strengthening Population and Family Planning Work and Stabilizing a Low Birthrate," March 2, 2000; Chinese version in State Birth Planning Commission, *Zhongguo Jihua Shengyu Nianjian, 2001 (China Family Planning Yearbook, 2001)* (Beijing: SBPC, 2001), pp. 33–36.

29. *Xinhua News*, "Number of Young Unmarrieds in China Increases," December 11, 2007 (*China Youth Daily* article), www.npfpc.gov.cn (accessed 2/25/08); also *China Daily*, "Family Planning Efforts," October 24, 2008 (Minister Li Bin statement), www.npfpc.gov.cn (accessed 11/10/08); Chen Hong and Hu Yinan, "Population Troubles Could Threaten Harmony," November 14, 2007 (Minister Zhang Weiqing speech), www.npfpc.gov.cn (accessed 2/25/08).

30. Decision, p. 7.

31. Willy Wo-Lap Lam, *Chinese Politics in the Hu Jintao Era,* pp. 34–62, esp. pp. 46–47.

32. Greenhalgh and Winckler, *Governing China's Population,* pp. 169–171.

33. Zhu Wei and Wang Shengxian, "China Helps over 80 Million Only-Child Families to Resist Reproductive Risks," April 9, 2008, www.npfpc.gov.cn (accessed 7/23/08).

34. Zhu Wei and Wang Shengxian, "China Helps over 80 Million."

35. Dahlman and Aubert, "China and the Knowledge Economy," p. 40.

36. Hu Yinan, "Baby Born with Birth Defects Every 30 Seconds," October 30, 2007, www.npfpc.gov.cn (accessed 2/25/08). Remarks of Jiang Fan, Deputy Head of the National Population and Family Planning Commission.

37. Hu Yinan, "Baby Born with Birth Defects."

38. Hu Yinan, "Baby Born with Birth Defects."

39. Decision, p. 5.

40. Willy Wo-Lap Lam, *Chinese Politics in the Hu Jintao Era,* p. 42.

41. China.org, "The New Five-Year Plan," November 9, 2005, www.china.org.cn (accessed 11/11/08).

42. China.org, "The New Five-Year Plan."

43. China.org, "The New Five-Year Plan."

44. China.org, "The New Five-Year Plan."

45. Li Ting, "National Forum of Directors of Population and Family Planning Commissions Held in Beijing," October 8, 2008, www.npfpc.gov.cn (accessed 11/20/08).

46. Evan A. Feigenbaum, *China's Techno-Warriors: National Security and Strategic Competition from the Nuclear to the Information Age* (Stanford: Stanford University Press, 2003), esp. chapter 1.

47. This argument is developed in various ways by Feigenbaum, *China's Techno-Warriors;* Hua Shiping, *Scientism and Humanism: Two Cultures in Post-Mao China (1978–1989)* (Albany, NY: State University of New York Press, 1995); and Wang Yeufarn, *China's Science and Technology Policy, 1949–1989* (Aldershot, UK: Ashgate, 1993), as well as by scholars who have traced the history of China's science policy.

48. The discussion above is based on Borge Bakken, *The Exemplary Society: Human Improvement, Social Control, and the Dangers of Modernity in China* (Oxford, UK: Oxford University Press, 2000), esp. chapter 2.

49. Song Jian, Tian Xueyuan, Yu Jingyuan, and Li Guangyuan, *Renkou yuce he renkou kongzhi (Population Projections and Population Control)* (Beijing: Renmin Chubanshe, 1982).

50. Donella H. Meadows, Dennis L. Meadows, Jorgen Randers, and William W. Behrens III, *The Limits to Growth: A Report for the Club of Rome's Project on the Predicament of Mankind* (New York: Universe, 1972); Mihajlo Mesarovic and Eduard Pestel, *Mankind at the Turning Point: The Second Report to the Club of Rome* (New York: E. P. Dutton, 1974).

51. G. J. Olsder and R. C. W. Strijbos, "Population Planning: A Distributed Time Optimal Control Problem," in Jean Cea, ed., *Lecture Notes in Computer Science; Optimization Techniques: Modeling and Optimization in the Service of Man, part I* (Berlin: Springer-Verlag, 1976), pp. 721–735; Huibert Kwakernaak, "Application of Control Theory to Population Policy," in A. Bensoussan and J. L. Lions, eds., *Lecture Notes in Control and Information Sciences: New Trends in Systems Analysis* (Berlin: Springer-Verlag, 1977), pp. 359–378

52. Song Jian, Tian Xueyuan, Li Guangyuan, and Yu Jingyuan, "Concerning the Issue of Our Country's Objective in Population Development" (in Chinese), *Renmin Ribao (People's Daily),* March 7, 1980, p. 5.

53. For the full story, see Susan Greenhalgh, *Just One Child: Science and Policy in Deng's China* (Berkeley: University of California Press, 2008).

54. Li Peng, "Speech While Receiving the Report of the National Conference of Directors of Family Planning Commissions (January 20, 1988)," in Tyrene White, ed., *Family Planning in China,* Special issue of *Chinese Sociology and Anthropology,* Spring 1992, pp. 64–79, quote on p. 66.

55. In the post-Mao era, China has become a virtual technocracy in which a majority of leaders at the middle and higher ranks are technical experts trained in natural science and/or engineering. In 2000, six of seven members of the Politburo's Standing Committee were engineers. In 1997, fully 70 to 80 percent of ministers, provincial party secretaries, and provincial governors were technocrats. See Li Cheng, *China's Leaders: The New Generation* (Lanham, MD: Rowman and Littlefield, 2001), pp. 25–26, 41.

56. The Chinese demographer Peng Xizhe has also noted how the population issue has been treated in much wider socioeconomic and environmental contexts in the 2000s, creating growing demand for demographic skills in urban planning, the design of social welfare systems, the restructuring of the education system, and so on. See Peng Xizhe, "Population Development Strategies: The New Thinking," in John Wong and Lai Hongyi, eds., *China into the Hu-Wen Era: Policy Initiatives and Challenges* (Hackensack, NJ: World Scientific, 2006), pp. 467–481.

57. Department of Publicity and Education, NPFPC, "'Three Designates Program' for NPFPC Was Unveiled with 21 New Additional Functions and Newly-Established Department," September 3, 2008, www.npfpc.gov.cn (accessed 11/10/08).

58. After the May 12, 2008 quake, the government sent teams of doctors to carry out reverse sterilization procedures. By mid-January 2009, according to official figures, 757 of the thousands of mothers who lost children were pregnant again. By the end of 2008, 5,724 mothers had received free reproductive services. Edward Wong, "China: Second Child for Quake Families," *New York Times*, January 17, 2009, p. A6.

59. Decision, p. 1.

60. Decision, p. 2

61. *China Population Press*, "Book of Research Report on National Population Strategy Published," October 19, 2007, www.npfpc.gov.cn (accessed 2/25/08). The other researchers were Jiang Zhenghua and Xu Kuangdi.

2. Creating Global Persons and a Global Society

1. See, for example, Nikolas Rose, *Powers of Freedom: Reframing Political Thought* (Cambridge, UK: Cambridge University Press, 1999), esp. chapter 6; and Peter Miller and Nikolas Rose, *Governing the Present: Administering Economic, Social and Personal Life* (Cambridge, UK: Polity, 2008).

2. See the contributions in Li Zhang and Aihwa Ong, eds., *Privatizing China: Socialism from Afar* (Ithaca, NY: Cornell University Press, 2008).

3. Susan Greenhalgh and Edwin A. Winckler, *Governing China's Population: From Leninist to Neoliberal Biopolitics* (henceforth *GCP*) (Stanford: Stanford University Press, 2005), esp. pp. 134, 190, 312–313.

4. Joseph Fewsmith, "Hu Jintao's Approach to Governance," in John Wong and Lai Hongyi, eds., *China into the Hu-Wen Era: Policy Initiatives and Challenges* (Hackensack, NJ: World Scientific, 2006), p. 97.

5. Aihwa Ong and Li Zhang, "Introduction: Privatizing China: Powers of the Self, Socialism from Afar," in Zhang and Ong, eds., *Privatizing China*, pp. 1–20, quote from p. 1.

6. Ong and Zhang, "Introduction," p. 4.

7. *GCP*. On the state's deliberate use of market mechanisms in policy and governance, see Xu Feng, "New Modes of Urban Governance: Building Community/ *Shequ* in Post-*Danwei* China," in André Laliberté and Marc Lanteigne, eds., *The Chinese Party-State in the 21st Century: Adaptation and the Reinvention of Legitimacy* (London: Routledge, 2008), pp. 22–38; David Bray, "Building 'Community': New Strategies of Governance in Urban China," *Economy and Society* 35 (2006), pp. 530–549; Lisa Hoffman, "Autonomous Choices and Patriotic Professionalism: On Governmentality in Late-Socialist China," *Economy and Society* 35 (2006), pp. 550–570; Gary Sigley, "Chinese Governmentalities: Government, Governance and the Socialist Market Economy," *Economy and Society* 35 (2006), pp. 487–508.

8. Winckler in *GCP*, p. 313.

9. This paragraph draws on *GCP*, pp. 213–214.

10. This paragraph draws on Joanna McMillan, *Sex, Science, and Morality in China* (London: Routledge, 2006); Elaine Jeffreys, ed., *Sex and Sexuality in China* (London: Routledge, 2006); Tze-Lan D. Sang, *The Emerging Lesbian: Female Same-Sex Desire in Modern China* (Chicago: University of Chicago Press, 2003); and James Farrer, *Opening Up: Youth Sex Culture and Market Reform in Shanghai* (Chicago: University of Chicago Press, 2002). On Shanghai, see McMillan, *Sex, Science, and Morality*; and Liu Jieyu, *Gender and Work in Urban China: Women Workers of the Unlucky Generation* (London: Routledge, 2007), esp. chapters 7 and 8.

11. This and the following two sections, which trace the history of quantity control and quality enhancement, are adapted from material in *GCP*.

12. A classic article on Maoist "voluntarism" is Ezra F. Vogel, "Voluntarism and Social Control," in Donald W. Treadgold, ed., *Soviet and Chinese Communism* (Seattle: University of Washington Press, 1967), pp. 168–184.

13. Nie Yilin and Robert J. Wyman, "The One-Child Policy in Shanghai: Acceptance and Internalization," *Population and Development Review* 31 (2005), pp. 313–336. For more on the early years of the one-child policy in the cities, see Cecelia Nathansen Milwertz, *Accepting Population Control: Urban Chinese Women and the One-Child Policy* (Richmond, Surrey, UK: Curzon, 1997); Elisabeth Croll, Delia Davin, and Penny Kane, eds., *China's One-Child Family Policy* (London: Macmillan, 1985); Margery Wolf, *Revolution Postponed: Women in Contemporary China* (Stanford: Stanford University Press, 1985); and Lisa Rofel,

Other Modernities: Gendered Yearnings in China after Socialism (Berkeley: University of California Press, 1999).

14. Nie and Wyman, "The One-Child Policy in Shanghai."

15. Milwertz, *Accepting Population Control.*

16. For more on rural birth planning in the 1980s and 1990s, see Tyrene White, *China's Longest Campaign: Birth Planning in the People's Republic, 1949–2005* (Ithaca, NY: Cornell University Press, 2006); Croll, Davin, and Kane, *China's One-Child Family Policy.* There is also a large journalistic literature on this period.

17. For field studies of the rural campaigns of the early 1990s, see Eric Mueggler, *The Age of Wild Ghosts: Memory, Violence, and Place in Southwest China* (Berkeley: University of California Press, 2001); Zhang Wei-guo, "Implementation of State Family Planning Programs in a Northern Chinese Village," *China Quarterly* 157 (1999), pp. 202–230; and Susan Greenhalgh, Zhu Chuzhu, and Li Nan, "Restraining Population Growth in Three Chinese Villages," *Population and Development Review* 10 (1994), pp. 365–395.

18. Zhang Hong, "From Resisting to 'Embracing'? The One-Child Policy: Understanding New Fertility Trends in a Central China Village," *China Quarterly* 192 (2007), pp. 855–875.

19. Charlotte Ikels, ed., *Filial Piety: Practice and Discourse in Contemporary East Asia* (Stanford: Stanford University Press, 2004).

20. Chu Junhong, "Prenatal Sex Determination and Sex-Selective Abortion in Rural Central China," *Population and Development Review* 27 (2001), pp. 259–281.

21. For the historical development through 2004, and the larger political context and significance of these post-2000 reforms, see *GCP*, esp. chapters 5 and 6. My discussion here emphasizes developments since then, bringing the account up to early 2009.

22. For the history of the seven don'ts, see *GCP*, pp. 190–191.

23. For the details, see, for example, Joan Kaufman, Zhang Erli, and Xie Zhenming, "Quality of Care in China: Scaling Up a Pilot Project into a National Reform Program," *Studies in Family Planning* 37 (2006), pp. 17–28.

24. The most significant recent example is "Decision of the Central Committee of the Communist Party of China and the State Council on Fully Enhancing [the] Population and Family Planning Program and Comprehensively Addressing Population Issues," January 22, 2007, at www.npfpc.gov.cn (accessed 3/23/07), p. 2.

25. According to two observers, the Hu–Wen administration's distinctive style of governance involves, among other things, projecting a populist, "pro-people" image and promoting numerous measures to improve the well-being of disadvantaged groups and underdeveloped regions; overhauling the party and government institutions for better governance; promoting the rule of law; fos-

tering high economic growth rates; and advocating China's "peaceful rise" and "peaceful development" in the international arena. See John Wong and Lai Hongyi, "The Hu-Wen New Deal," in Wong and Lai, eds., *China into the Hu-Wen Era,* esp. pp. 8–9. On the ongoing transformation from a management-based to a service-based approach to governance, see Zou Keyuan, "Rule of Law and Governance," in Wong and Lai, eds., *China into the Hu-Wen Era,* pp. 191–216. All of these larger regime priorities are reflected in the population/reproduction arena.

26. Li Ting, "'Three Systems' Establish Guide to Care for Families Practicing Family Planning: Population and Family Planning System Comprehensively Advances Construction of Benefit-oriented Family Planning System," September 1, 2008, www.npfpc.gov.cn (accessed 11/10/08).

27. Department of Publicity and Education, NPFPC, "'Three Designates Program' for NPFPC Was Unveiled with 21 New Additional Functions and Newly-Established Department," September 3, 2008, www.npfpc.gov.cn (accessed 11/10/08).

28. General Office, NPFPC, "Speech by Wang Pei'an, Vice Minister of NPFPC at the Second Workshop on Family Planning Administrative Law Enforcement of Anyang City, Henan Province," November 15, 2007, www.npfpc.gov.cn (accessed 2/25/08).

29. Willy Wo-Lap Lam, *Chinese Politics in the Hu Jintao Era: New Leaders, New Challenges* (Armonk, NY: M. E. Sharpe, 2006), pp. 72–73.

30. This point is elaborated in *GCP,* pp. 166–169.

31. Xu Feng, "New Modes of Urban Governance: Building Community/*shequ* in Post-*danwei* China," in André Laliberté and Marc Lanteigne, eds., *The Chinese Party-State in the 21st Century,* pp. 22–38.

32. *Xinhua News,* "China Bans Stiff Family Planning Slogans," August 5, 2007, www.npfpc.gov.cn (accessed 12/2/08); Shan Juan, "Family Planning Posters Toned Down," October 12, 2007, www.npfpc.gov.cn (accessed 12/2/08).

33. *Xinhua News,* "China Bans Stiff Slogans." These changes are part of a broader campaign by the regime to clean up party propaganda so as to burnish the public image of the CCP. For that larger effort, see Zheng Yongnian and Lye Liang Fook, "Re-making the Party's Image: Challenges for the Propaganda Department," in Wong and Lai, eds., *China into the Hu-Wen Era,* pp. 119–151.

34. Michael Palmer, "Transforming Family Law in Post-Deng China: Marriage, Divorce and Reproduction," *China Quarterly* 191 (2007), pp. 675–698. Whereas promising experiments are underway in the new terrain of "population," which is being interpreted to mean, broadly, social policy, in the field of reproduction, the persistence of old thinking and institutions seems to be creating obstacles to humanizing reform. Those barriers are reflected in the 2001 law.

35. M. Giovanna Merli, Zhenchao Qian, and Herbert F. Smith, "Adaptation of a Political Bureaucracy to Economic and Institutional Change under Socialism: The Chinese State Family Planning System," *Politics and Society* 32 (2004), pp. 231–256; Yunxiang Yan, *Private Life under Socialism: Love, Intimacy, and Family Change in a Chinese Village, 1949–1999* (Stanford: Stanford University Press, 2003).

36. On the quality project, see Terry Woronov, *Transforming the Future: "Quality" Children for the Chinese Nation* (PhD dissertation, University of Chicago, 2002); and Susan Champagne, *Producing the Intelligent Child: Intelligence and the Child Rearing Discourse in the People's Republic of China* (PhD dissertation, Stanford University, 1992). The origins of the Chinese concept *suzhi* are ably explored by Andrew Kipnis, "Suzhi: A Keyword Approach," *China Quarterly* 186 (2006), pp. 295–313.

37. Suzanne Z. Gottschang, *Hospitalizing Motherhood: Medicine and Modernity in a Beijing Hospital* (Durham, NC: Duke University Press, forthcoming). For more on the gendered expectations surrounding reproduction, see Emily Honig and Gail Hershatter, *Personal Voices: Chinese Women in the 1980s* (Stanford: Stanford University Press, 1988), and Gail Hershatter, *Women in China's Long 20th Century* (Berkeley: University of California Press, 2007).

38. Some examples are Liu Longyan and Zhang Jianhua, eds., *Quality Births and Fetal Education Work* (Beijing: New World Press, 1999) (in Chinese); and Qu Mujie, ed., *Doing Ability Games: Games to Enhance Intelligence, Ages 0–6* (Beijing: China Women's Press, 2001) (in Chinese).

39. See note 36, and Gottschang, *Hospitalizing Motherhood*.

40. James L. Watson, ed., *Golden Arches East: McDonald's in East Asia* (Stanford: Stanford University Press, 1997); Eriberto P. Lozada, Jr., "Globalized Childhood? Kentucky Fried Chicken in Beijing," in Jing Jun, ed., *Feeding China's Little Emperors: Food, Children, and Social Change* (Stanford: Stanford University Press, 2000), pp. 114–134.

41. Vanessa L. Fong, *Only Hope: Coming of Age under China's One-Child Policy* (Stanford: Stanford University Press, 2004); "Parent-Child Communication Problems and the Perceived Inadequacies of Chinese Only-Children," *Ethos* 35 (2007), pp. 85–127.

42. Nie and Wyman, "The One-Child Policy," pp. 326–327.

43. Liu, *Gender and Work*, p. 134.

44. Vanessa L. Fong, "Morality, Cosmopolitanism, or Academic Attainment? Discourses on 'Quality' and Urban Chinese-Only-Children's Claims to Ideal Personhood," *City and Society* 19 (2007), pp. 86–113.

45. Wang Gan, "'Net-Moms'—A New Place and a New Identity: Parent Discussion Forums on the Internet in China," in Tim Oakes and Louisa Schein, eds., *Translocal China: Linkages, Identities, and the Reimagining of Space* (London: Routledge, 2006), pp. 155–165.

46. Michelle Leung, "Couples Crave for Olympic Babies," October 13, 2007, www.npfpc.gov.cn (accessed 2/25/08).

47. Andrew Jacobs, "On Good-Luck Day, 17,000 Beijing Couples Tie Knot," *New York Times*, August 9, 2008, p. A9.

48. Palmer, "Transforming Family Law," pp. 688–689.

49. *Xinhua News*, "Beijing to Fine Celebrities Who Break Family Planning Rule," January 21, 2008, www.npfpc.gov.cn (accessed 2/25/08).

50. Gottschang, *Hospitalizing Motherhood*.

51. NPFPC, "New Services for Would-be Moms," December 20, 2007, www.npfpc.gov.cn (accessed 2/25/08).

52. Judith Banister, "Shortage of Girls in China Today," *Journal of Population Research* 21 (2004), pp. 19–45.

53. Carl J. Dahlman and Jean-Eric Aubert, *China and the Knowledge Economy: Seizing the 21st Century* (Washington, DC: World Bank, 2001), esp. chapters 3 and 5.

54. Created in 1990, the HDI is used by the United Nations Development Program to rank all U.N. member nations annually by a single standard of "human development," understood as the process of widening people's options and opportunities to gain education, health care, income, work, and so on. The measure has been criticized on a number of grounds—redundancy, narrowness, neglect of the environment, and so on—yet continues to play a major role in international assessments of nations' relative social welfare.

55. For the estimates, see Susan Greenhalgh, "Making Up China's 'Black Population,'" in Simon Szreter, Hania Sholkamy, and A. Dharmalingam, eds., *Categories and Contexts: Anthropological and Historical Studies in Critical Demography* (Oxford, UK: Oxford University Press, 2004), pp. 148–172.

56. For more on the fate of "black children," see Kay Ann Johnson, *Wanting a Daughter, Needing a Son* (St. Paul, MN: Yeong and Yeong, 2004).

57. For an in-depth look at state efforts to improve the "quality" of women and enhance their competitiveness in the market economy, see Ellen R. Judd, *The Chinese Women's Movement Between State and Market* (Stanford: Stanford University Press, 2002).

58. On the lives of gay couples and parents, see, for example, Jeffreys, *Sex and Sexuality in China*; McMillan, *Sex, Science, and Morality*; and Farrer, *Opening Up*.

59. Howard W. French, "Single Mothers in China Forge a Difficult Path," *New York Times*, April 6, 2008, pp. A5, 11. See also People.com, "Storm in a Test Tube," February 3, 2004, http://english.people.com.cn (accessed 7/25/08).

60. *China Daily*, "Family Planning Efforts," October 24, 2008, npfpc.gov.cn (accessed 11/10/08).

61. Cai Yong and William Lavely, "Child Sex Ratios and Their Regional Variation," in Zhao Zhongwei and Guo Fei, eds., *Transition and Challenge: China's Population at the Beginning of the 21st Century* (Oxford, UK: Oxford University Press, 2007), pp. 108–123.

62. Dudley L. Poston and Karen S. Glover, "China's Demographic Destiny: Marriage Market Implications for the Twenty-first Century," in Dudley L. Poston, Che-Fu Lee, Chiung-Fang Chang, Sherry L. McKibben, and Carol S. Walther, eds., *Fertility, Family Planning, and Population Policy in China* (New York: Routledge, 2006), pp. 167–181.

63. *China Daily,* "Family Planning Efforts."

64. An overview of the birth commission's projects on gender equity and women's empowerment can be found at www.npfpc.gov.cn/en/genderpro.htm.

65. John C. Caldwell and Zhao Zhongwei, "China's Demography in Perspective," in Zhao and Guo, eds., *Transition and Challenge,* pp. 283–284.

66. Zhao Zhongwei and Guo Fei, "Introduction," in Zhao and Guo, eds., *Transition and Challenge,* pp. 7–9.

67. Decision, pp. 7–8.

68. Li Ting, "'Three Systems.'"

69. Richard Jackson and Neil Howe, *The Graying of the Middle Kingdom: The Demographics and Economics of Retirement Policy in China* (Washington, DC: Center for Strategic and International Studies; and Newark, NJ: Prudential Foundation, 2004).

3. Strengthening China's Party-State and Place in the World

1. David Shambaugh, *The Modern Chinese State* (Cambridge, UK: Cambridge University Press, 2000), and *China's Communist Party: Atrophy and Adaptation* (Washington, DC: Woodrow Wilson Press, 2008).

2. See, for example, Chien-min Chao and Bruce J. Dickson, eds., *Remaking the Chinese State: Strategies, Society, and Security* (London: Routledge, 2001), esp. the introductory chapter by the editors; and contributions in David S. Shambaugh, ed., *Is China Unstable?* (Armonk, NY: M. E. Sharpe, 2000).

3. For interesting discussions of these more positive views of the regime, see, for example, Shambaugh, *China's Communist Party;* David M. Lampton, *The Three Faces of Chinese Power: Might, Money, and Minds* (Berkeley: University of California Press, 2008); André Laliberté and Marc Lanteigne, eds., *The Chinese Party-State in the 21st Century: Adaptation and the Reinvention of Legitimacy* (London: Routledge, 2009); and Kjeld Erik Brodsgaard and Zheng Yongnian, eds., *The Chinese Communist Party in Reform* (London: Routledge, 2006).

4. *Governing China's Population* documents the rise in state capacity that has resulted from the governance of China's population. See esp. chapters 3 through 6, written by my coauthor, a political scientist. Susan Greenhalgh and Edwin A. Winckler, *Governing China's Population* (Stanford: Stanford University Press, 2005).

5. This paragraph is adapted from Greenhalgh and Winckler, *Governing China's Population,* p. 285.

6. The numbers in this paragraph come from Department of Personnel, NPFPC, "The Fourth Bulletin on Personnel Statistics of National Population and Family Planning System," April 16, 2007, www.npfpc.gov.cn (accessed 12/2/08).

7. A wide-ranging discussion of the 2001 law and its significance can be found in Edwin A. Winckler, "Chinese Reproductive Policy at the Turn of the Millennium: Dynamic Stability," *Population and Development Review* 28 (2002), pp. 379–418.

8. General Office, NPFPC, "Speech by Wang Pei'an, Vice Minister of NPFPC at the Second Workshop on Family Planning Administrative Law Enforcement of Anyang City, Henan Province," November 15, 2007, www.npfpc.gov.cn (accessed 2/25/08).

9. General Office, NPFPC, "Speech by Wang "Pei'an."

10. An excellent discussion of population legislation is Thomas Scharping, *Birth Control in China 1949–2000: Population Policy and Demographic Development* (London: Curzon, 2003), pp. 83–105. These numbers are from p. 90. For a useful English-language database on population laws and regulations, see UNESCAP, "Population and Family Planning Laws, Policies and Regulations: China," www.unescap.org. On family law more generally, see Michael Palmer, "Transforming Family Law in Post-Deng China: Marriage, Divorce and Reproduction," *China Quarterly* 191 (2007), pp. 675–698.

11. See esp. Dali Yang, *Remaking the Chinese Leviathan: Market Transition and the Politics of Governance in China* (Stanford: Stanford University Press, 2004).

12. This paragraph is adapted from Greenhalgh and Winckler, *Governing China's Population,* p. 288.

13. *Xinhua News,* "China Bans Stiff Family Planning Slogans," August 5, 2007, www.npfpc.gov.cn (accessed 12/2/08).

14. "People's Republic of China Law on Population and Birth Planning," *Population and Development Review* 28 (2002), pp. 579–585.

15. "Decision of the Central Committee of the Communist Party of China and the State Council on Fully Enhancing [the] Population and Family Planning Program and Comprehensively Addressing Population Issues," January 22, 2007, at www.npfpc.gov.cn (accessed 3/23/07).

16. Adriana Petryna, *Life Exposed: Biological Citizens After Chernobyl* (Princeton, NJ: Princeton University Press, 2002).

17. The birth project has helped to legitimate the party's right to continued rule in part by emphasizing the party's caring concern for the nation and the Chinese people.

18. Lampton, *Three Faces,* p. 118.

19. André Laliberté and Marc Lanteigne, "The Issue of Challenges to the Legitimacy of CCP Rule," in Laliberté and Lanteigne, eds., *Chinese Party-State,* pp. 1–21.

20. Decision, p. 2.

21. Nina Halpern, "Making Economic Policy: The Influence of Economists," in U.S. Congress, Joint Economic Committee, *China's Economy Looks Toward the Year 2000, vol. 1, The Four Modernizations* (Washington, DC: U.S. Government Printing Office, 1986), pp. 132–146; and "Scientific Decision Making: The Organization of Expert Advice in Post-Mao China," in Denis Fred Simon and Merle Goldman, eds., *Science and Technology in Post-Mao China* (Cambridge, MA: Harvard University, Council on East Asian Studies, 1989), pp. 157–174; and Carol Lee Hamrin, *China and the Challenge of the Future: Changing Political Patterns* (Boulder, CO: Westview, 1990).

22. Lampton, *Three Faces*, p. 121.

23. Mark Leonard, *What Does China Think?* (New York: Public Affairs, Perseus, 2008).

24. Willy Wo-Lap Lam, *Chinese Politics in the Hu Jintao Era: New Leaders, New Challenges* (Armonk, NY: M. E. Sharpe, 2006), esp. pp. 40–45.

25. For the full story, see Susan Greenhalgh, *Just One Child: Science and Policy in Deng's China* (Berkeley: University of California Press, 2008).

26. The following is based on conversations with social demographers in Beijing, Shanghai, and Xi'an conducted between 1985 and 2003.

27. Interview file, 11/16/99, Beijing.

28. Interview file, 7/4/93, Beijing.

29. Interview file, 11/16/99, 11/29/99, Beijing.

30. See, for example, Zeng Yi, "Options for Fertility Policy Transition in China," *Population and Development Review* 33 (2007), pp. 215–246.

31. Lampton, *Three Faces*, p. 121.

32. *Xinhua News*, "Brief Introduction to China's Cabinet Members," March 18, 2008, Chinadaily.com. (accessed 1/21/09).

33. "United Nations Population Award to Indira Gandhi and Qian Xinzhong," *Population and Development Review* 9 (1983), pp. 747–753, quote on p. 751.

34. "United Nations Population Award," p. 751.

35. Barbara B. Crane and Jason L. Finkle, "The United States, China, and the United Nations Population Fund: Dynamics of US Policymaking," *Population and Development Review* 15 (1989), pp. 23–59, esp. p. 38.

36. See statements on the UNFPA Web site, www.unfpa.org. On the Obama administration's decision, see "U.S. Resumption of UNFPA Funding to Boost Women's Health and Rights," March 12, 2009, www.unfpa.org (accessed 3/31/09).

37. Lisa de Cardona and Dee Brooks, "Issues Arising in Coercive Population Control Claims: Survey of Board of Immigration Appeals and Federal Court Decisions," *Immigration Law Advisor* 1(9), September 2007, www.usdoj.gov (accessed 8/6/09).

38. Interview file, 3/12/02, Canberra.

39. Interview file, 11/4/98, 4/15/99, 6/24/99, 10/14/99, Princeton, NJ.

40. John C. Caldwell and Zhao Zhongwei, "China's Demography in Perspective," in Zhao Zhongwei and Guo Fei, eds., *Transition and Challenge: China's Population at the Beginning of the 21st Century* (Oxford, UK: Oxford University Press, 2007), pp. 271–285, esp. p. 285.

41. James Reynolds, "Chinese Challenge One-Child Policy," *BBC News*, May 27, 2007, www.news.bbc.co.uk (accessed 3/31/09).

42. Joseph Kahn, "Harsh Birth Control Steps Fuel Violence in China," *New York Times*, May 22, 2007, p. A12; Joseph Kahn, "Chinese Police Arrest 28 in Riots Against Family Planning Laws," *New York Times*, May 24, 2007, p. A13.

43. This paragraph is based on discussions in Lampton, *Three Faces*, esp. p. 118, and Leonard, *What Does China Think?*

44. David Barboza, "News Media Run by China Look Abroad for Growth," *New York Times*, January 15, 2009, p. A6.

45. Lampton, *Three Faces*.

46. Joshua Kurlantzick, *Charm Offensive: How China's Soft Power Is Transforming the World* (New Haven: Yale University Press, 2008); also Lampton, *Three Faces*, p. 29.

47. Caldwell and Zhao, "China's Demography."

48. See especially Zhang Hong, "From Resisting to 'Embracing'? The One-Child Policy: Understanding New Fertility Trends in a Central China Village," *China Quarterly* 192 (2007), pp. 855–875; Yun Yanxiang, *Private Life under Socialism: Love, Intimacy, and Family Change in a Chinese Village, 1949–1999* (Stanford: Stanford University Press, 2003).

49. Gu Baochang, Wang Feng, Guo Zhigang, and Zhang Erli, "China's Local and National Fertility Policies at the End of the Twentieth Century," *Population and Development Review* 33 (2007), pp. 129–147.

50. On the doctoring of population data and its consequences, see Thomas Scharping, "The Politics of Numbers: Fertility Statistics in Recent Decades," in Zhao and Guo, eds., *Transition and Challenge*, pp. 34–53.

51. See, for example, Leonard, *What Does China Think?*; Lampton, *Three Faces*, pp. 20–25; Michael Pillsbury, *China Debates the Future Security Environment* (Washington, DC: National Defense University Press, 2000).

52. Hu Angang and Men Honghua, "The Rise of Modern China (1980–2000): Comprehensive National Power and Grand Strategy," *Strategy and Management* 3 (2002). A convenient English translation is available under the title "The Rising of Modern China: Comprehensive National Power and Grand Strategy," 2004, at www.irchina.org/en. All page numbers below come from this version. This quote from p. 2.

53. Leonard, *What Does China Think?*; Lampton, *Three Faces*.

54. Sujian Guo, ed., *China's "Peaceful Rise" in the 21st Century: Domestic and International Conditions* (Hampshire, UK: Ashgate, 2006).

55. For a discussion of these limitations, see Lampton, *Three Faces*, p. 23.

56. Lampton, *Three Faces*, p. 23.

57. Hu and Men, "The Rising of Modern China," p. 27.

58. Wang Feng and Andrew Mason, "The Demographic Factor in China's Transitions," in Loren Brandt and Thomas Rawski, eds., *China's Great Economic Transformations* (Cambridge, UK: Cambridge University Press, 2008), pp. 136–166.

59. Wang and Mason argue that if it can "get its institutions right"—a big if— China might enjoy a second demographic dividend as the population ages. For the details, see Wang Feng and Andrew Mason, "Population Ageing: Challenges, Opportunities, and Institutions," in Zhao and Guo, eds., *Transition and Challenge*, pp. 177–196.

60. For the policy consensus, see Lampton, *Three Faces*, p. 24.

Index

abortion: coerced, 49, 88, 101, 105; New Right crusade against, 5. *See also* sex-selective abortion
"administration by law," 85
Adoption Law, 1991, rev. 1998, 84
adult literacy: China versus other nations, 71t, 72
age gap, 41
age structure: changes in, 111; pyramid-shaped, 17, 18f
aging parents, abandonment of, 52
aging: accelerated, 1, 2, 24, 77, 105–106, 112; problem as reproductive modernization consequence, xiii; without social security, 107
Aird, John S., 5–6
Aiwha Ong, 39
anatomy as social destiny, gender roles and, 43

"babies of fortune," 66
baby theft, laws dealing with, 84
bachelor population, growth of, 76, 107
"backward" masses, transformation of, 58, 81
"backward" persons: bodies and minds of, 20; excessive numbers of, 16–17, 44; individuals labeled as, xiii; overview of, 73–75
backwardness, saving nation from, 82
Banister, Judith, 116n10
biocapital, 12
biocitizens, 12
biogovernance: global rise, role in, xi; importance, increasing of, 12; term usage, 11–12
biological entity, population as, 12, 42, 81
biology, governing through, 87–89

biopolitics: of population project, 15, 21; term, xi, 11
biopower, 87–88
biotechnologies, 12
"birth according to law," 56
"birth according to plan," 56
birth cadres: local elections of, 55; managing, 87; reforms adopted by, 57; women's reproduction regulated through, 47–48
birth defects, 26, 91
"birth peak," 17–18, 19
birth planning: birth crackdown, 19–20; commissions and committees, hierarchy of, 82; compliance rewarded, 76, 91; mandatory, 45; science of, 43; state assistance and economic incentives, 54; state role in, 16; term usage, 2, 115n3
birth program: categories of persons, new, 40, 41; documentary productivity of, 86; governing experiments within, 41; human-centered reforms in, 51; maternal and early child health promotion role of, 59; reforms of, 55–56, 57, 104, 123n34
"black children" *(hei haizi)*, 74
Bush, George H. W., 102
Bush, George W., 6–7, 102

celebrity parents with two or more children, 66–67
center *(zhongyang)* (defined), xii
child development milestones, 60–61
child health services, 54
child intelligence, development of, 60–61
child quality project, 58–64
child trafficking, 7

childbearing: preferences, falling, 104; restrictions and rules on, x, 24

childless persons, 43

child-rearing: globalizing economy technological resources role in, 66; as scientific enterprise, 60. *See also* child quality project

children: economic costs of, 49, 51–52; food and nutrition of, 62; health and education, rising levels of, 69; investment in, 61–62; legislation protecting, 84

China's National Strategy for Population Development (2004–2007), 34, 36

Chinese Communist Party (CCP) legitimacy, 92–94

Chinese Model of Development, 95

citizen rights, 34

class struggle: during Mao administration, 42; rejection of, 16

"client satisfaction" (term), 53

"client-centered reform" (term), 53

Clinton, Bill, 102

Club of Rome, 31

"coercion and commandism" *(qiangzhi mingling)*, 44, 86. *See also* physical force

coercive campaigns: phasing out, gradual of, 23, 52–53, 104; in rural areas, 48–51

coercion story: irrelevance, increasing of, 8–9; origin and rise of, 3–6, 101–103; overview of, x–xi, 2–3; persistence of, 6–8; person-making in, 41; science and engineering story more important than, 37

"coercively persuasive" techniques, 45

"comprehensive governance," 28

"comprehensive national competitiveness," 26

Comprehensive National Power (CNP): assessing, xiv; boosting, 80–81, 100; China and other nations compared, 110t; overview of, 108–109

Confucianism, 29

Connelly, Matthew, 2–3

Constitution of the PRC, 1978 and 1982, 84

Criminal Law, 1979 (rev. 1997), 84

crisis-crackdown narrative: continuation of, 35–36; in population politics, 19–20

Cuellar, Javier-Perez de, 101

Cultural Revolution: aftermath of, 44, 47; mothering after, 61–62; overview of, 42

cybernetics: logic of, 29; or control theory, 31. *See also* population cybernetics

daughter-only policy. *See* 1.5-child policy

daughters: preference, growing for (rural), 51; preference, growing for (urban), 47; role of, 49

Dean, Mitchell, 117n17

Decision on Fully Enhancing the Population and Family Planning Program and Comprehensively Addressing Population Issues, 2007: adoption of, 21; population as threat doctrine, 36; population growth addressed in, 22; rural girl-child families, 91

defective births, preventing, 20

Democracy Model, 95

demographic dividend, 112

demographic engineering, 30–35

demographic information, national database of, 34

demographic problem, 16–18

demographic research centers, 83

demographic skills, growing demand for, 34, 120n56

demography (term), 10

Deng Xiaoping: advisors of, 30; economic growth promoted by, 16; party-state power buildup under, 82; population policies of, 16–17, 20, 95–96, 99, 103; science and technology promoted by, 17, 42, 94

"deviant" persons: categories of, 74–75; individuals labeled as, xiii

disadvantaged groups: measures to aid, 54, 122n25; needs, addressing, 23

economic governance: overview of, 14–16; quantity and quality aspects, 16–20

economic growth: achievement of, 111–112; birth program combined with, 104; continued, promise of, 92; emphasis on, consequences of, 21, 108; human potential, means to developing, 27; human-centered approach to, 54, 55, 122–123n25; population growth outpacing, 16–17, 117n18; push for, 16

economic-to-social governance transition, 14–16

economy-first model, xiii

education: advances in, 72; advancing own, 27–28; child quality promotion role of, 58; promotion of, 21

elderly: care of, 24, 47, 62, 77, 106 (*see also* old-age support); increase in, 77; legislation protecting, 84

Eleventh Five-Year Plan for National
Economic and Social Development
(2006–2010), 21, 27, 34, 113
embryonic development chart, 60f
emergency management, 25
engineering, Chinese leaders trained in, 32,
120n55
environment: degradation of, 20; population
growth effect on, 22–23; protection of,
55, 92
ethnography: of Chinese party-state, xiv;
population governance and, 10–12; of state
population project, 13–14
*Eugenic Births and Fetal Education Work
(Yousheng: Taijiao Gongcheng)*, 59–60
eugenics: law and legislation, 84; national
"organism" improvement through, 42;
population quality and, 20; scope of, 58

family planning (birth planning):
organizations and personnel devoted to,
83–84; population reduced to, 9; term
usage, 2, 115n3; in third-world countries,
28; voluntary nature, shift toward, 57;
women-friendly and human-centered, 99
family-size preference: among rich and
famous, 66–67, 68; marketization of, 49–52;
rural, 49, 52; urban, 47, 48
Fatal Misconception, 2–3
fertility decline: below replacement level,
22, 41, 51, 68; causes of, 112; coerced, 51;
developmental opportunity due to, 111;
gender preference and, 52; global, 103, 104;
policy change advocates citing, 36; social
problems caused by/consequences of, 23, 24;
success in achieving, 1
fertility drugs, 105
fertility rise, counter-measures against, 50
Fewsmith, Joseph, 38
Foucault, Michel: sexuality and governance
studies of, 11; state governmentalization
described by, 15
"Four Modernizations," 17

gays, 74–75
gender equality: promotion of, 76, 107
gender gap: consequences of, 75–76; as
reproductive modernization consequence,
xiii, 1, 41
gender roles, 43–44, 49

genetic engineering, 58–59; birth defects,
preventing through, 26
genetics, 12
girls: elimination of, 105; sex selection practice
consequences for, 52
girls, baby: abandonment of, 77; killing of, 3, 5,
7, 101; violence against, 50
global citizens, consumerist versions of,
63–64
global competition, 25–26
global economy: education role in, 72; human
capital role in, 94
global good citizenship, 99–108
global personhood: foreign goods and services,
consumption as avenue toward, 63–64;
scientific norms guiding, 37
global position: impact on party-state, 79–80;
population governance influence on, 80
global power: boosting, xiv; population role in,
42; transformation into, 9, 14
global rise: categories of persons essential
to, 40; other nations' role in China's, xiv;
population governance role in, xv, 13, 100;
population role in, 15; social problems
threatening, 41
global society, problems of, 68–78
"good mother": concept of, 58, 67; creation of,
59–62; role and duties of, 40
Governing China's Population, xiv–xv, 38,
39–40
governmentality perspective: overview of, xi,
12; population politics focus broadened
through, xii
governmentalization: neoliberal, 39; of
population, works on, xv; of state, 15
grass-roots democracy, 55
Great Leap Forward: mass starvation during,
48
Guangxi riot, 105

Hao Haidong, 67
"hard power," ix, 109–110, 111
"harmonious society," 55, 93, 95
Harvard Girl Liu Ying, 63
haves and have-nots, gaps between, 55, 67,
104
health: advancing own, 27; child quality
promotion role of, 58
HIV/AIDS epidemic, 25
Hu Angang, 109, 111

Hu Jintao: market dynamics and neoliberalism applied by, 39; scientific concept of development promoted by, 27, 34

Hu Jintao-Wen Jiabao administration: birth program reforms under, 41; "harmonious society" promoted by, 55, 95; human governance under, xii; human-centered governance under, 53–54; neoliberalism under, 38–39; population problem reframing by, xii; systems approach to population backed by, 32, 34

Hu Yaobang, 45

human capital: aggregate measure of, xiv; defined, x; development based on, 20–21; factors affecting, 111; global economy role of, 94; and global greatness, 109–113; improving, challenges of, 26; population as, 113; strengthening, 21, 26–28

human development: aggregate measure of, xiv; population problem reframed in terms of, 23; promotion of, 26–28, 34–35, 93–94, 113

human development index (HDI): background on, 72, 125n54; China and other nations compared, 72–73, 73t

human governance: emergence of, 9, 34, 94; future, 113; ideas and techniques, new of, 87

human rights abuses, 101, 103, 104, 105

"human-centered development": promoting, 26

human-centered governance: marketization and program reform aimed at, 41; obstacles to, 57, 123n34; rise of, 52–57; techniques of, xii–xiii

ideational power (term), 106

Immigration and Nationality Act (U.S.), 1996, 102

India: China's greatness compared to that of, xiv; comparative studies on, xiv; urban areas, population proportion in, 69

individual responsibility: instilling, state role in, 39; shift toward, 87; Western emphasis on, 38

infant and child mortality rates, 69, 70t

"informed choice," 53, 99

international family planning movement, 2–3

Jiang Zemin, 39

Just One Child (2008), xv

Kentucky Fried Chicken, 63

knowledge-based economy: global shift toward, 21; quality population for, 25–26; social and human development role in creating, 28

Kurlantzick, Joshua, ix

labor force: children as labor source, 68; high-quality, development of, 20; quality, promoting, 25–26, 27; shaping of, 13; transformation of, 58

labor-intensive development, shift away from, 20–21

Lam, Willy Wo-Lap, 95

Lampton, David M., 106

later-longer-fewer policy *(wanxishao)*, 16

Law on Protection of Minors, 1991, 84

Leninism, 29

Leninist instruments of control, erosion of, 79

Leninist neoliberalism: concept defined, 38–39; emergence of, 40; modifications of, 54

Leonard, Mark, 95

Li Bin, 98–99

Li Peng, 32

Li Zhang, 39

life expectancy: China versus other nations, 69, 70t, 72; rise in, 77

life sciences, state promotion of, 12

"low-quality" citizens, 74

Malthus population growth problem, 16–17, 117n18

Mao administration: advisors of, 30; legacy of, 42, 44; population growth not controlled by, 81

Maoism, 29

market forces: population governance role of, 59; quality children creation role of, 63–64

market regimes, Western versus Chinese, 38

market socialism, 41

marketization, 38–39, 112

marketizing reforms: state power and, 79; subject-creation as component of, 38

"market-socialist subjects," creating: marketization and program reform role in, 41; rural birth work, 51–57

market-state relationship, neoliberalism and, 40

marriage: late, encouraging, 16; need for, 94; norms, rejection of, 74; one-child generation attitude toward, 64; polyandrous, 76; prospects, gender gap effect on, 76; restrictions on, 59
Marriage Law, 1982, 84; 2001 revision of, 57
Mason, Andrew, 111–112
mass media (Western): coercion story construction role of, 3–5; human rights abuses documented by, 101; population policy coverage, declining of, 7
McDonald's, 63
Medium- to Long-term Science and Technology Development Plan, 34
Men Honghua, 109, 111
migrant population, 22
modern society problems, 68–73
modernization: categories of persons essential to, 40; Chinese Communist Party (CCP) role in, 17; crises of, 43; environment-economy-society system role in facilitating, 29–30; of population, 81; population project role in, 13, 14, 113; science and technology role in, 30–31; social problems in wake of, 41; threats to, 41
Mosher, Stephen, 6, 116n10

national power, boosting, ix–x, xi
natural resources: population growth effect on, 22–23; protection of, 92
natural science, 32, 120n55. *See also* cybernetics
neoliberalism: defined, 38; establishment of, 39; market, reliance on as principle of, 55; shift toward, 87
"net-mom," 66
New Right coalition, 5–6
New York Times, 3–5, 103

Obama, Barack, 102
old-age (social) security system: developing and improving, 24; family care as component of, 77
old-age support: children role in, 49, 51, 62, 68; crisis, impending in, 78; crisis, response to, 36; economic, lack of, 1; employers as source of, 47; rural, 78; state role in, 54, 91, 94
Olympic baby, 66
1.5-child policy: adoption of, 19, 50; areas with, 2, 115n2

one-child family: acceptance, popular of, 48; state propaganda concerning, 45, 46f, 112
one-child generation as adults, 64–65
one-child policy: continuation of, 35–36, 57, 90, 104; current media coverage of, 7–8; economic aspects of, 108; ethical aspects of, 100; future fate, possible of, 22, 98, 99, 103, 107; genetics rise spurred by, 12; human costs of, 98; irrelevance, increasing of, 8–9; one-child generation attitude toward, 64–65; origins and establishment of, xv, 18–19, 32, 44, 45, 99; resistance to, 7, 37, 48, 49, 50, 93, 101, 104, 105; science behind, 95–96; slogans promoting, 89–90; social consequences of, 1–2; violation of, 66–67; Western media coverage of, 3, 5
one-child policy enforcement: rural, 48–51; shift in rules and, 14; softening of, 98; urban, 45, 47–48
"one-vote veto" system, 50
Open Letter of September 1980, 17

parenthood, one-child generation attitude toward, 64–65
parenting, books on, 60
party slogans, 89–90
party-state: governing capacity of, 79–80; stronger, more capable, 81–89
"peaceful development," 54, 109, 122–123n25
"peaceful rise," 54, 109, 122–123n25
Peng Peiyun, 96–97, 98
Peng Xizhe, 34, 120n56
people-centered governance. *See* human-centered governance
personhood, creating, 91–92
persons, creation of new, 37–38
physical force: official prohibition of, 44–45; use of, 49–50, 101
political Center. *See also* center (*zhongyang*): defined, xii; function of, 85; research on, xiii
population, definition and scope of, 9–10, 15, 29, 42, 81
Population and Birth Planning Commission, 22–23
Population and Birth Planning Law, 2001, 57, 67
population control: coercion story emphasis on, 8; social and human costs of, 23
Population Control Theory, 31
population crisis, permanent, 93

population cybernetics: limitations of, 96; overview of, 29; rise of, 30–35

population discourse, 89–94

population, framings of: changes in, 13; identification of, 13; as modernization crisis, 43; overview of, xi; "population security," 25; scope of, 10–11; social and human development approach, 23; in socialist construction era, 16; state control over, 14–15

population governance: analysis coverage, lack of, ix, x; capacity, growing, 86–87; changing approach to, 16; combined approaches to, 2, 115n3; complexity of, 81; economic aspects of, 16–20; ethnographic aspects of, 10–12; future, 113; global position influenced by, 80; global rise, role in, xv; law and legislation, 84–85; Leninism and neoliberalism combined in, 39–40; participation, broadening of, 59, 94, 112; reframing of, xi; responsibility, sense as motivation behind, 100; scope of, xii, 15; shift away from, 9, 21; as social and human governance, 22–28; as social systems engineering, 28–36; state as agent of, 8, 15; from state-centric to multicentric, 41; Western interest, declining in, xii

population growth: continuing, 22; control of, 82; economic growth outstripped by, 16–17, 117n18; future projections of, 19f; global, addressing, 100; location and group variations in, 22; lowering, 43, 100, 104; Mao's failure to control, 81; official position concerning, 22; social effects of, 14; unstoppable, fear of, 18

population management, organizations facilitating, 82–84, 83t

population policy: compliance rewarded, 76, 91–92; crisis narrative underlying, 35–36; expansion of, 82; international influences on, 99; noncompliance penalties, 91; problems, legislation addressing, 85; slogans promoting, 89–90; studies of, x

population policy enforcement: categories of, 91–92; through Maoist mobilizational campaign, 44

population quality: China and other nations compared, xiv, 70t–71t; definition and overview of, x; entities involved with, 28; investment in, 113; physical and mental, 43; promotion of, 21, 41

population quantity: China and other nations compared, xiv; limitation on, 8; mathematical propositions, ix–x (2XP: math. prop's.); quality linked to, 20; reduced emphasis on, 41; restrictions on, 17, 21 (*see also* one-child policy); stabilization of, 86

population science: emergence of, 17, 42–43; logic of, 13; term usage, 10

"population security," 25

poverty population, 22

pregnancy: activities to avoid during, 61f; concealing, 49; healthy, scientific, promotion of, 59–60, 60f

prenatal genetic screening, counseling and diagnosis, 26

prenatal sex determination, 24

private selves, emerging: differentiation of, 40; market as force behind, 39; overview of, xiii; promotion of, xii

Program for Chinese Children's Development, 62

propaganda and education (*xuanquan jiaoyu*): clean-up and humanization of, 55–56; modern person, creation of, 112; as population policy enforcement tool, 44, 49, 100

"putting people first" (*yiren weiben*), 23

Qian Xuesen: population award given to, 101; science and technology ideas influenced by, 30–31, 96

"quality child": cultivating, 62–64; overview of, 40; producing, 58–59

"quality of care," 53, 99

quality persons, 27–28

quality population, 25–26

quality (*suzhi*) (concept), x, 20, 58, 65

race (quality question) as biological entity, 42

Reagan, Ronald, 6, 102

"Red China," West depiction of, 3

"reform and opening up" (*gaige kaifang*), 16

reproduction: culture of, 65; ethnographic approach to, 10, 11; micromanagement, state retreat from, 34; modernization of, categories of persons involved in, 40; social-scientific understandings of, 56–57; state control over, 32, 90

reproductive freedom, 5

reproductive health: concern for, 97; science of, 43; services, 54

reproductive insecurity: overview and government response to, 25; population and, 24–25

reproductive norms: promotion of, 10; rejection of, 74

reproductive rights violations, 8, 107

reproductive selves (or subjects): autonomy of, 64–65; characteristics of, 41; creation of, 40, 44, 56, 58; enacting, 66

reproductive technology, 42

"reproductive woman," 40

"revolutionary-socialist subjects," creation of: socialist revolution role of, 45; urban quantity control, 45, 47–48; volunteerism as tool in, 41

right-to-life agenda, 6

rule of law, 54–55

rural China: birth planning and preferential treatment for, 76; birth work, 51–57; couples, old-age support for, 54, 77–78; girl-child families, legislation concerning, 91

science: politicized, dangers of, 95–96; and scientific logics, political effects of, 12

science and technology: advanced, dependence on, 27; global rise, role in, 9, 12; modernization role of, 17; nation's biological body governed through, 15; political life, role in, xi; population problems, solving with, 81; promotion of, 21; religion of, 30–31; state promotion of, xi, 12, 94; Western influence on, 42

"scientific concept of development": definition and overview of, 26–27; harmonious society based on, 95; human development promotion through, 34–35, 113; informatization and computerization role in, 34

self, fostering of: governance techniques, 104; market-oriented techniques, role in, 41

self-governing subject: 27–28, 37, 39, 40, 55, 56, 59, 64–65

selfhood and society, 38–39

service orientation: in health care, 54; success, measuring, challenges of, 57

"seven don'ts *(qige bujun)*, 52–53

Severe Acute Respiratory Syndrome (SARS), 25

sex determination, prenatal, 52

sex preference, 23–24

sex ratio among children, 75–76

sex ratio at birth: addressing, 97, 105; distortion of, 36; one-child policy and, 1, 107; sex preference as factor in, 24

sex-selective abortion: as family formation tool, 52; legislation concerning, 91; one-child policy and, 107; prohibition on, 97; sex ratio affected by, 24

sexual norms, 43

sexually transmitted diseases (STDs), 25

Shaanxi: coercion campaign in, 49–50; old-age support problems in, 52; slogans displayed in, 90

Sichuan earthquake, 2008, 35, 120n58

single children, health and education of, 59, 62–63

single children, injury or death of: assistance to parents following, 25, 54, 91; births, new allowed following, 35, 120n58

Slaughter of the Innocents, 5–6

Smith, Christopher, 7

Social Compensation Fee, 67, 68

social Darwinism, 29

social development: elevation of, 55; labor force quality impact on, 26; population problem reframed in terms of, 23

social engineering, 57

social governance: emergence of, 9; emphasis on, 23; ethnography of, xiv; popular participation in, 55; problems, new of, 23; state role in managing, 39–41; techniques, new of, xii

"social harmony and stability": labor force quality impact on, 26; preserving, challenges of, 20–21

social insurance schemes, state role in, 91

social policy: expansion of, 82; population as part of, x

social problems: economic growth emphasis as cause of, 21; fertility reduction as cause of, 23; official perception of, 14; sociopolitical change as cause of, 15

social scientific reasonings, 56–57

social scientists, larger voice for, 96–99

social stability, 92, 93; risks, addressing, 25; sex ratio at birth, distorted as threat to, 36

social systems engineering, 28–36

socialist legality, 84–86

socialist revolution: categories of persons essential to, 40; during Mao administration, 42; individual contributors sought to support, 45; rejection of, 16
"soft power," ix, 106–108, 109
Song Jian, 31–32
sons: old-age support, declining by, 24, 52; preference, reducing, attempts at, 76; role of, 49
State Birth Planning Commission: methods, shift in, 53; purpose of, 82
"state guidance, mass voluntarism," 29, 100
state: power, 79, 80, 82; science, 42–44; strengthening, 82–84
sterilization campaign: as population policy enforcement tool, 49, 88; resistance to, 19
sterilization procedures, reversal of, 35, 120n58
subject-creation, state-sponsored: as modernization component, 40; overview of, 38, 41
subjectification, 56
systems engineering, 29, 34
systems theory, 29, 31

"taking people as primary" *(yiren weizhu)* (term), 53
"tangible strategic resources" model, 109–110
technocracy, xi, 32, 33f, 94–95, 98, 120n55
technology. *See* science and technology
techno-scientific state, 42; population and, 94–99
three-child family, rural preference for, 49
three-child policy, areas with, 2, 115n2
"two transformations" *(liangge zhuanbian)*, 23, 98
two-child family: in rural areas, 19, 49 (pref. for); as urban ideal, 47, 48
two-child policy, 16; areas with, 2, 115n2; experiments, 98

underdeveloped regions, 54, 122n25
unequal society, 75–78
United Nations Population Fund (UNFPA), 5, 6
United States: China's greatness compared to that of, xiv, 80–81; relations with China, 101–102; view of China as coercive state, 3
unmarried men, rise in, 24
unmarried mothers, 43

"unmodern" persons: concept, 41; societal norms rejected by, 74–75
urban areas: below replacement level, 68; population proportion in, 68–69; quantity control, 45, 47–48

vital politics: effects of, 79; as hybrid formation, 39–40; money role in, 40, 65–68; population as, 9–14; population project strategic ends in, 13; quality promotion role in, 58; shifts, critical in, 41; term usage, xi, 11–12
"voluntarism": definition and overview of, 44–45; as one-child policy enforcement mechanism, 47, 100; revolutionary-socialist subject formation through Maoist, 41; women's reproduction and, 48

Wang Feng, 111–112
"Washington Consensus," 38
Washington Post, 3–5, 103
Wen Jiabao. *See* Hu Jintao-Wen Jiabao administration
Western view of China: as coercive state, x–xi, 101–103; interest, declining in population policy, xii; science and technology role ignored in, 37
What Does China Think?, 95
Winckler, Edwin A., xiv–xv, 38, 39–40
women: discrimination, protection against, 77; family economy role in, 112; kidnapping and trafficking of, 76, 77, 84; physical force against, 50–51; sex selection practice consequences for, 52
women's health: as birth defect prevention component, 26; emphasis, new on, 23, 54; mandatory checks for, 59; reproductive health, 53, 99
women's reproduction: monitoring and management of, 47–48; shaping own, 104
workplace *(danwei)* system, population policy enforcement role of, 47
Wu, Harry, 6–7

Zhang Weiqing: one-child policy, statements on, 7; "population security" addressed by, 25
Zhao Baige, 7
Zheng Bijian, ix–x
Zhou Enlai, advisors of, 30

Harvard University Press is a member of Green Press Initiative (greenpressinitiative.org), a nonprofit organization working to help publishers and printers increase their use of recycled paper and decrease their use of fiber derived from endangered forests. This book was printed on recycled paper containing 30% post-consumer waste and processed chlorine free.